THE NORTH YORKSHIRE MOORS RAILWAY

THE NORTH YORKSHIRE MOORS RAILWAY

Michael A Vanns

PEN & SWORD
TRANSPORT

First published in Great Britain in 2017
and re-issued in this format in 2022 by
Pen & Sword Transport
An imprint of
Pen & Sword Books Ltd
Yorkshire – Philadelphia

Copyright © Michael A Vanns, 2017, 2022

ISBN 9781399077248

Typeset in Palatino by Milepost 92½
Printed and bound by Replika Press Pvt. Ltd.

Pen & Sword Books Limited incorporates the imprints of Atlas,
Archaeology, Aviation, Discovery, Family History, Fiction, History,
Maritime, Military, Military Classics, Politics, Select, Transport, True
Crime, Air World, Frontline Publishing, Leo Cooper, Remember When,
Seaforth Publishing, The Praetorian Press, Wharncliffe Local History,
Wharncliffe Transport, Wharncliffe True Crime, White Owl and After
the Battle.

For a complete list of Pen & Sword titles please contact

PEN & SWORD BOOKS LIMITED
47 Church Street, Barnsley, South Yorkshire, S70 2AS, England
E-mail: enquiries@pen-and-sword.co.uk
Website: www.pen-and-sword.co.uk
or
PEN AND SWORD BOOKS
1950 Lawrence Rd, Havertown, PA 19083, USA
E-mail: Uspen-and-sword@casematepublishers.com
Website: www.penandswordbooks.com

Contents

Preface

This book in the series 'Heritage Railway Guides' has been written for all those who want to know something of the story behind one of Britain's major heritage railways. It looks at the line through the North Yorkshire Moors taken over by enthusiasts, putting it into the broader history of the companies that originally built and subsequently ran it. As a guide, it cannot examine every aspect of the railway's history, and for those who want to delve further, there is a selective bibliography. The last chapter covering the preservation years reflects the views of the author, which might not necessarily coincide with those of the people who have worked, or continue to work, for the organisations mentioned.

This book is dedicated to all those who have worked for and supported the North Yorkshire Moors Railway and kept the trains running.

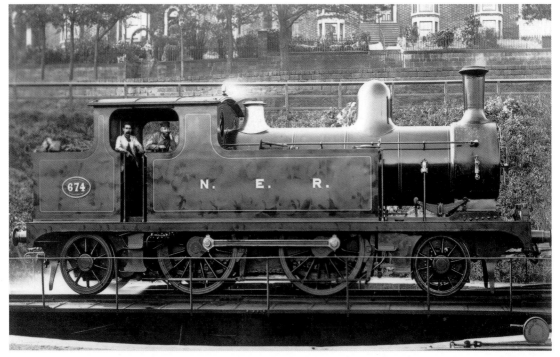

Polished to perfection, North Eastern Railway Class A 2-4-2 No. 674 standing on the turntable at Whitby in the first years of the twentieth century. Sixty of this type of locomotive were built to the designs of the company's Locomotive Superintendent, T.W. Worsdell, who was in office between 1885 and 1890. (Real Photos)

The up starting signal at Goathland station, a fine example made for the North Eastern Railway (NER) by McKenzie & Holland of Worcester. It was recovered by the North Yorkshire Moors Railway (NYMR) from Barlby Crossing, Selby and erected at Goathland in 1972 and then repositioned to the location illustrated here in 1987. (Author)

Introduction

One of the most interesting aspects of creating the three books in the Heritage Railway series was trying to account for the reasons why the railways have developed in the way they have after they were taken out of British Railways ownership. Obviously there have been many factors, ranging from the physical constraints of the route to the resources available to maintain and run trains. But perhaps the fundamentals of preservation and operation, and the way these two have been balanced out over the years, have influenced the appearance of heritage railways more than any management, staffing or financial issues. Because the initial aim of the Main Line Steam Trust was the preservation of a section of main line, it could be argued that the goal for the Great Central Railway in Leicestershire has been more towards the recreation of a main line with appropriate track layouts and signalling, compared to the original aim of the North York Moors Historical Railway Trust (NYMHRT), formed in 1972, that was 'To advance the education of the public in the history and development of railway locomotion by the maintenance in working order of the historic and scenic railway line between the towns of Grosmont and Pickering.'

Although this statement has been considerably refined over the years, especially since the organisation became a 'registered museum' requiring the words 'preservation' and 'conservation' to appear in the aims of the Trust, that initial emphasis on the running of trains does help explain why many original features on the North Yorkshire Moors Railway (NYMR) have been sacrificed since 1967 to provide better facilities for passengers and the maintenance of locomotives and carriages. It helps explain why so many metal-clad sheds have been erected and why track maintenance and renewal and signalling on the line have developed in the way they have. It is also important to record that the NYMR has been run as a heritage line for longer than it was in the hands of the LNER and British Railways combined, and those businesses also had to adapt to changing circumstances. But perhaps more importantly, with the exception of the original Whitby & Pickering Railway Company, no organisation before the NYMR had to operate the line as a self-contained unit. Locomotive and carriage maintenance did not have to be carried out and stock stored permanently somewhere between Pickering and Grosmont. Civil engineering and permanent way equipment and heavy lifting gear did not have to be accommodated either, all that being brought in from elsewhere when needed. In many ways, since 1967 the NYMR has had to become a self-contained LNER. All those issues and many more have combined to make the NYMR what it is today and it makes a fascinating story.

Repatriated from Greece in 1984, restored and named *Dame Vera Lynn*, War Department 2-10-0 is on the 1 in 49 climb between Grosmont and Goathland during the summer of 1989. (Author's collection)

Early Days to Best Years

When the Whitby & Pickering Railway (W&PR) was completed in 1836, it was already old-fashioned. Since 1830 the Liverpool & Manchester Railway (L&MR) had been running trains on a double train main line, demonstrating emphatically that the future was steam powered, and within a few years (1838), an even more ambitious railway – the London & Birmingham Railway (L&BR) – would be completed, one that in the twenty-first century still remains the spine of Britain's railway network.

When it opened, horses pulled single coaches on the single track W&PR at almost the same speeds as stage coaches on the country's network of turnpike roads, whereas on the L&MR and L&BR, coaches were coupled together to form trains capable of transporting many more people than a single stage coach and they were pulled by modern steam locomotives that travelled at three or four times the speed of horses.

The W&PR had much more in common with the Stockton & Darlington Railway (S&DR) opened in 1825 than either the L&MR or L&BR. On the mainly single track S&DR, there were sections where wagons were attached to ropes to run up and down inclined planes, and other places where either horses or primitive steam locomotives were employed to pull the trains. The W&PR never used steam engines, but the reason it shared so many other characteristics with the S&DR was due to the fact both lines were engineered by George Stephenson. The initial surveys and costings for the L&MR had also been his responsibility, but due to inaccuracies in both these areas he had been replaced. Much of the credit for the design and use of steam locomotives on that line must also be placed elsewhere, in this instance with his son, Robert Stephenson, who went on to engineer the L&BR. Nevertheless, despite his blunders, and his son's growing reputation, George Stephenson still remained throughout the 1830s the leading advocate on the great benefits railways could bring to all parts of the country. He was the man everyone turned to on all matters relating to railways and this is why the promoters of the W&PR sought his advice.

Whitby & Pickering Railway

The impetus for building a line through the North Yorkshire Moors had come from Whitby. Traditionally, that community had looked to the North Sea for its trade and prosperity, but at the beginning of the nineteenth century, the whaling and boat-building industries

The wooden bridge over the Murk Esk immediately north of Grosmont Tunnel from an engraving by G. Dodgson in 'Scenery of the Whitby & Pickering Railway', 1836. Although the railway was brand new, the artist presented the scene as a romantic landscape, the bridge depicted as though spanning the moat of the rustic castle gatehouse beyond, in reality the railway tunnel entrance. (P. Waller collection)

were in decline, which also adversely affected other trades. The days of Captain Cook's voyages of discovery in wooden ships built at Whitby were over. The town, however, was still handling sea-borne coal traffic, and conscious of the growing network of railways connecting the collieries with the sea a few miles further north-west, local businessmen, many of whom had financially supported the S&DR, were considering whether to promote their own line to join it, or to look to create a new outlet for coal traffic southwards through Pickering.

By 1831, both alternatives had attracted influential supporters based on some preliminary surveys and cost analyses, and it was at this point that an approach was made to George Stephenson for his opinion on the best option. His view was that it would not be cost effective to build a railway to establish a new north-west trading route when it was still possible to sail from Whitby to Middlesbrough and link up with the existing railway network there. He did believe there were considerable benefits to connecting Whitby to Pickering by a railway, benefits he characteristically over-estimated. He stated that there could be a significant increase in finished goods and of raw materials such as coal, limestone and timber available to those communities along its route, leading to a reduction in the costs of these commodities. A new railway would also stimulate the development of hitherto unproductive land. Many of the same arguments were used by other railway companies in the 1830s and then again during the later 'Railway Mania' of 1845/6 to justify the building of new lines.

Stephenson estimated the projected annual income of the railway would be in the region of £13,000, mainly from mineral traffic, more than covering the costs of building the 24 mile (38.6km) line, which he confidently declared would be only £2,000 a mile.

Stephenson's advocacy of the Pickering route was crucial, and a prospectus for the W&PR was issued and funds raised for a bill to be presented for the Parliamentary Session of 1833. The plans and estimates must have

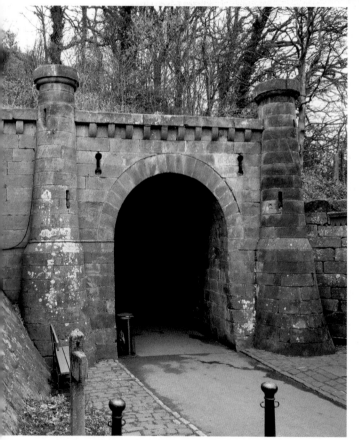

The **southern portal** of the original Whitby & Pickering Railway (W&PR) tunnel at Grosmont. This was one of the earliest examples of the decorative tunnel entrance, a feature that became very popular in railway architecture in the 1830s, '40s and '50s. In the early days of railway travel, many passengers were transported in open carriages, and so decorating tunnel entrances in this way was intended to reassure them of the solidity and, therefore, safety, of the structure they were about to enter. It also made a statement of the taste of the company that built them, confirming their connection and respect for the past. (Author)

been sufficiently convincing because the W&PR gained its Royal Assent in May 1833. Stephenson was appointed engineer, delegating supervision of the construction work, which began in September of that year, to Frederick Swanwick. This young engineer was involved in many of the older man's other projects, so the translation of the broad-brush predictions into the details of actual civil engineering was left to the contractors. Very quickly construction estimates were exceeded, the costs per mile doubling, largely due to an increase in the price of iron, and the W&PR was plunged into perpetual debt.

The unforgiving topography of the moors also stretched the budget. Immediately outside of Whitby, although the River Esk was diverted to save two expensive river crossings, in the 6 miles (9.7km) between there and what later became Grosmont, the river still had to be bridged ten times. At the latter, the rocky River Musk Esk had to be crossed and a 120yds (110m) long tunnel driven through Lease Rigg hill.

Once clear of the tunnel, the river valley was regained and followed to Beck Hole, where the line parted company from it to begin a 500yds (457m) ascent to Goathland village. This was the Goathland inclined plane. Almost 2 miles (3.5km) south of the incline, the railway reached its summit and entered Fen Bog, a tract of land as treacherous as Chat Moss on the L&MR and requiring similar methods of construction to get the line through to Newton Dale. The line continued to twist and turn as it followed the natural outline of this valley, dropping rapidly down towards the site of Levisham station, at one point at a gradient of 1 in 49. Beyond there the line was straight for almost 2 miles (3.5km) but still contained within the remote dale. Then, after crossing from the east to the west side of Pickering Beck, the line once again began to

each coach ran downhill as far as it could by gravity, its speed controlled by the guard applying his brake, until horses were once again attached for the final pull into Pickering.

For the majority of the local population, who had no experience of the L&MR, the new railway must have been an attractive novelty because in August 1836 some 4,200 people travelled along the line. Statistics like this are difficult for historians to interpret without comparisons, so as a way of trying to put this into context, in 1839, the first year of operation of the single track, but steam-powered, Midland Counties Railway (MCR) between Nottingham and Derby, (both places with much larger populations than either Whitby or Pickering) it was calculated that on average, 10,000 passengers were carried every month.

When the Whitby & Pickering Railway opened in 1836, its way of working had more in common with horse-drawn stage coaches on turnpike trust roads than the more up to date Liverpool & Manchester Railway or London & Birmingham Railway. Consequently, apart from at Pickering and Whitby, there were no other recognisable 'passenger stations' on its route. In 1836, fares were advertised between Pickering, Raindale, 'Incline Station House', Beck Hole, Tunnel Inn and Sleights Bridge. By 1838, Levisham Road had been added to the list of stops and this detail from an Edwardian postcard shows what might have been an existing building there adapted for railway use. The platform was a post-1845 addition. (Commercial postcard, author's collection)

Perhaps of more significance than the transportation of curious passengers was the establishment of new industries stimulated by the opening of the W&PR. The stone quarrying around Grosmont has already been mentioned, but when iron ore was discovered during the excavation of the tunnel there, commercial quarrying soon followed. The Whitby & Grosmont Lime Co. built lime kilns close by, and both industries helped turn the growing settlement around the Tunnel Inn into the town of Grosmont.

The York & North Midland Railway

Despite these encouraging developments the W&PR Company was never able to trade its way out of debt. The anomaly of having clauses in its original Act that both allowed and prohibited the use of steam locomotives was never resolved and this reflected an organisation both out of step with the times and lacking funds for improvements.

It was during this period of stagnation that the York & North Midland Railway (Y&NMR) entered the story. This

company's line opened in 1840 between Normanton, just outside Leeds, and York, one of the links in a chain of lines that formed the first continuous railway route between London and York via Derby. The company's chairman was George Hudson, a wealthy and ambitious York draper who by the mid-1840s had acquired the unofficial title of 'The Railway King' because of his considerable influence in current railway affairs. It was Hudson who pushed for the amalgamation in 1844 of the three railway companies centred on Derby to form the Midland Railway (MR) that became one of the country's most powerful organisations.

George Stephenson had engineered both the line north of Derby and the

A 1950s view of Grosmont looking north from above the railway tunnels. Just to the right in the middle of the photograph, with the hipped roof, is the Tunnel Inn. It was a short walk from there for passengers using the initial service in 1836 of two trains daily in either direction over the entire route, with the addition of a train to and from Beck Hole each day. Given the current pronunciation of Grosmont, it is interesting to see it spelt as 'Growmond' in a timetable of 1838. The tall chimney in the background belonged to the 1870s brickworks. (Author's collection)

Rillington Junction station looking north-east on 18 April 1952, over twenty years after it had closed to passengers in 1930. It still retains the characteristic overall roof designed by G.T. Andrews and provided at many other York & North Midland Railway (Y&NMR) stations, including Whitby and Pickering. The junction to the Whitby & Pickering line was just beyond the end of the platforms. (Author's collection)

Y&NMR, and Hudson had turned to him again when seeking to push a line from York to Scarborough in 1840. Hudson also had aspirations of transforming Whitby into a holiday destination, the West Cliff area of the town on the side of the estuary where the railway station was located being ripe for new developments. Key to his vision was creating a connection between the projected Scarborough line and the W&PR. The plans for the York to Scarborough line received Parliamentary approval in 1844, and by the time the Royal Assent for the purchase of the W&PR by the Y&NMR was secured a year later on 30 June 1845, the Scarborough line was only seven days from opening to traffic, having been completed in only one year three days since gaining its Act, a breath-taking achievement. On the same day the link from Rillington Junction (just north of Malton on the Scarborough line) to

Pickering was brought into use, passenger services starting in October that year.

In February 1846, the Y&NMR started work to bring the W&PR up to the standards of the rest of its double track lines. Although the W&PR had been laid with only a single track, sufficient land had been acquired by the company for two parallel lines. Timber bridges were replaced – a fine stone arch being erected at Grosmont where a new tunnel was also excavated – and the whole route was relaid with heavier rails so it could be worked by steam locomotives. The only section where this was not possible was on the inclined plane that was retained, a new stationary steam engine at Goathland replacing the original self-acting gravity system.

The down home signal (a North Eastern Railway example) at Marishes Road station between Rillington Junction and Pickering. The station was one of three on this Y&NMR link when completed in July 1845, but soon became the only one to remain open. It closed on 8 March 1965, the month this photograph was taken, looking towards Pickering. (Author's collection)

The existing W&PR buildings there and at Levisham remained in railway use, whilst new permanent stations were established at Whitby, Grosmont, Ruswarp, Sleights and Pickering. Handsome new stone buildings and roofs that covered both platforms and track were erected at Whitby and Pickering, the main entrance to the former enhanced by a five arch portico. A stone two road engine shed was built immediately south-west of that station with a new stone goods shed on the opposite side of the line. The equivalent structures at Pickering, both south of the station, were smaller, the goods shed made of stone, and the single road engine shed of brick. Cottages for employees were also provided at various places along the line, all the new buildings and the masonry structures designed by George Townsend Andrews, the York architect who was making his mark on many railways in the north-east of

England in this period. From September 1846, Pickering and Levisham were served by steam hauled trains, and then in June 1847 steam locomotives started to work in and out of Whitby station. Although anyone travelling the whole length of the line did not have to change trains, the inclined plane effectively divided the route into two separate operational sections. Nevertheless, the times of journeys between Whitby and Pickering improved from the 2hr 30min to 3 hours of horse-drawn days, to just 1hr 30min going south and 1hr 25min going north. One of the earliest timetables for the summer of 1848 shows three trains a day providing this service, with the addition of an extra southbound train from Pickering to York

A view looking north at Saltersgate at the north end of Newton Dale, with the trees of Wilden Moor to the left and Lockton High Moor and Fen Moor in the background. Although the train, heading for Levisham station, was travelling too fast for the slow shutter speed of Mr Smith's camera, the double track of the Y&NMR's 1845 improvements is well shown in this 1920s photograph. (S. Smith commercial postcard, author's collection)

A clear view through the Y&NMR double track tunnel at Grosmont from the new 1845 station there. Compared with the 'gothic folly' entrance to the single track W&PR tunnel of the previous decade (hidden by the locomotive), the new tunnel relied on its massive stone blocks rather than any overt ornamentation to assure travellers of its durability. (R.N. Joanes, 20 April 1961)

Levisham station was almost 2 miles (3.5km) from Levisham village, the connecting road between the two seen sweeping out of Newton Dale in this detail from a pre-First World War postcard. Also prominent in this view is Grove House, set in a large rectangle of tree-backed ground, once the home of the Rowntree family of York. In 2016 it was for sale for £850,000. (J.W. Malton commercial postcard, author's collection)

Looking north up Park Street, Pickering, with the Y&NMR's railway station unchanged when this postcard was printed and circulated by Lilywhite Ltd in the early 1920s. Number 12 Park Street was purchased by the North Yorkshire Moors Railway (NYMR) in 1990 to provide accommodation for its head office and for volunteers. (Commercial postcard, author's collection)

A detail of a postcard posted from Whitby to West Hartlepool on 26 April 1908. It shows Sleights station on a quiet, summer day, a poster advertising Scarborough Flower Show propped up next to the entrance to the booking office. The attractive station building with its understated Tudor features and decorative, timber barge-boards, was designed by G.T. Andrews for the Y&NMR as part of that company's upgrading of the facilities on the line after 1845. (Commercial postcard, author's collection)

The new 1845 station at Pickering, like those at Rillington and Whitby, was provided with a wrought-iron, timber and slate roof that covered both platforms. It survived until 1952, two years after this photograph was taken. (Lens of Sutton Association/66383)

and two extra northbound returning services. A journey between Whitby and York could be completed in between 3hr to 3hr 15min.

All these Y&NMR improvements had been carried out during the 'Railway Mania' years of 1845/6, when hundreds of new railway projects had been floated to tempt investors. During this period of frenetic speculation, fortunes were made but many more people lost money – both small and large amounts. For others, reputations were also lost, including that of George Hudson. Having helped inflate the bubble, he suffered an investigation into his business affairs that exposed some dubious practices and led to his very public disgrace in 1849. In complete contrast, two years earlier in 1847, Robert Stephenson had become the Conservative Party's MP for Whitby, a position he held until his death in 1859.

The North Eastern Railway

Following the 'Railway Mania', there was a period of reflection and retrenchment, and eventually in 1854, as a means to secure the finances of the four railway companies serving York and the north-east, the North Eastern Railway (NER) was formed by amalgamation. One of the companies absorbed was the Y&NMR.

The line between Rillington Junction and Whitby then became a small part of the new NER's empire. The pattern of services remained the same for a few years until the inconvenience of the Goathland incline could no longer be tolerated. By the end of the 1850s it was an anachronism. In 1860 the NER drew up plans to build a new double track line from just under half a mile (805m) south of Grosmont Tunnel, where it would curve away from the old route, climbing continuously up the eastern edge of the Murk Esk valley to a point immediately above Beck Hole, in order to reach the rocky path of the Eller Beck from where this tributary would be followed to Goathland Mill. Once clear of this valley, the new route would rejoin the existing line at Moorgates, 1.25miles (2km) south of Goathland. These 'deviation' plans were approved by Parliament in 1861 and construction work started in the summer of the following year.

The whole route required some careful civil engineering not always obvious to ordinary travellers. The ledge cut for the railway immediately north of Beck Hole featured long stretches of retaining wall made up of large, beautifully dressed, stone blocks, laid at a 'batter', that is,

leaning away from the line at a slight angle so as to form a brace to the land behind the wall. The section that followed Eller Beck was particularly challenging as access for materials and space in which to drive through the line and work effectively was very restricted. The section of line on the approach to Goathland Mill was cut into the hillside above and on the east side of Eller Beck, requiring another length of stone retaining wall. The new station adjacent to Goathland Mill was perched on an impressive stone plinth, the station buildings and goods shed constructed of matching stone blocks and reached via a new bridge over the

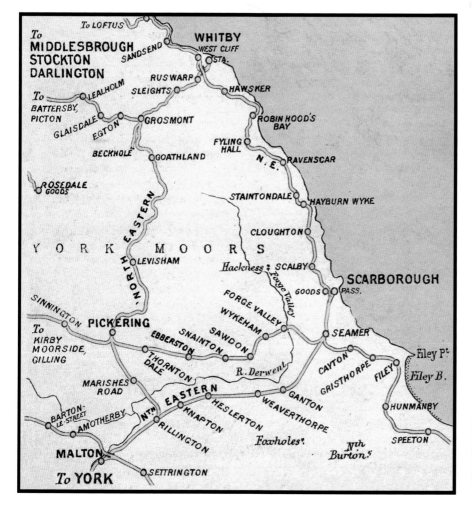

A detail from the Railway Clearing House's map of the rail network of mainland Britain immediately after the First World War. (Author's collection)

beck. Between Grosmont and Goathland Mill the route was laid out with a ruling gradient of 1 in 49, one that George Stephenson and even his son, Robert, would have considered too steep to be worked by steam locomotives, and over the years, many trains had to be 'banked' up this incline – that is, pushed from behind by another locomotive.

The 'Goathland Deviation' of 1865 led to the erection of some impressive stone structures, including this one – bridge No. 31 – at Water Ark. The bridge crossed Eller Beck at a skew and although it cannot be seen in this Edwardian photograph, all the stones in the arch were beautifully cut at the appropriate angle and laid with very thin mortar joints. Beauty for operational requirements. (Ross of Whitby commercial postcard, author's collection)

The new 'deviation' came into use on 1 July 1865, finally eliminating the 1836 Goathland inclined plane. The improvement was long overdue as there had been a number of accidents on the incline, the last two both caused by the rope breaking. In October 1861 a goods train being hauled up the incline had broken free, fortunately without human injury, but then on 10 February 1864 two lives were lost with thirteen others injured, when the rope snapped on the descent of five passenger carriages.

The deviation not only improved safety, it also reduced journey times even further. The four trains serving all stations between Pickering and Whitby could complete the journey in about 1hr 10min, the two non-stop services taking only 50min. The equivalent two express trains in the opposite direction also took 50min, with the remaining four stopping trains averaging a few minutes over the hour.

After 1865, the original route between Grosmont and the foot of the incline remained open to serve the small communities at Esk Valley and Beck Hole, but southwards, tracks were removed. The incline was only used again for railway purposes very briefly during 1872 when special narrow gauge track with Fell's patent central rail was installed so that a Manning, Wardle & Co. steam locomotive destined for Brazil could be tested in June of that year.

Three months after the deviation opened, Grosmont became a junction, with the completion of a line from Picton, on the Northallerton to Stockton branch. The route had been promoted by the North Yorkshire & Cleveland Railway (NY&CR) in 1854, but had taken over ten years to reach Grosmont from the west. This was the first of four new lines built to connect with the railway between Whitby and Rillington Junction. In April 1875, a line opened connecting Pickering to Gilling via Kirby Moorside to the west, and then in May 1882, from the

A detail from another Edwardian postcard, this one showing the 1865 Goathland station with two very noticeable chimney stack additions indicating a recent reorganisation of the internal rooms. The design of the main station building was also used for those on the Grosmont–Castleton section of line opened in October 1865, three months after Goathland. To the right, only its roof visible through the trees, is Goathland Mill next to the wrought-iron bridge over Eller Beck. (Author's collection)

No book about the North Yorkshire Moors Railway would be complete without the reproduction of this familiar photograph. It was taken in 1893 and shows one of the NER's 'Whitby bogies' designed by locomotive superintendent, Edward Fletcher, especially for working the line after the 'Goathland Deviation' had been completed. This particular engine was posed for its portrait in front of the houses along Windsor Terrace, Whitby. (F. Moore)

In this Edwardian photograph of Goathland station, the only addition to the suite of buildings provided when it opened in 1865 was the signalbox that came into use on 1 May 1876. The prominent 'V' in the hillside behind the goods shed and station buildings marks the course of Eller Beck, descending rapidly with the railway towards Grosmont. In 1999 the NYMR converted the goods shed into a refreshment room, a very successful adaptation. (Commercial postcard, author's collection)

An afternoon train at Darnholm in the 1920s climbing the 1 in 49 gradient of the 1865 'Goathland Deviation' between Grosmont and Goathland. The engine is crossing bridge No. 28, its stone arch of 1865 replaced in red brick. Once preserved steam locomotives started to work this section of line again from the 1970s, Darnholm became very popular with railway photographers. (S. Smith commercial postcard, author's collection)

east, another line came in from Seamer (the 'Forge Valley Line'), both branches linking into the W&PR at Mill Lane just south of Pickering station.

A few years later, Whitby was linked to two new routes, which both involved major civil engineering work. In December 1883 the first to open came in from the west, the last section of a route originally promoted by the Whitby, Redcar & Middlesbrough Union Railway (WR&MUR) in the middle of the 1860s. A new station was built in the developing West Cliff area of the town, and then the single track line plunged south, dropping down Airy Hill at 1 in 50 before turning through 180 degrees to head due north, running parallel with the W&PR until joining it at Bog Hill junction within sight of the 1847 terminus.

Another signalbox brought into use in the mid 1870s to control trains on the line by using the absolute block system, was High Mill at the north end of Pickering station. It is seen here on the extreme left next to the engine turntable, with the masonry remains of the thirteenth century Pickering Castle prominent in the background. (S. Smith commercial postcard, author's collection)

The other new line, which came in from Scarborough via Robin Hood's Bay, opened shortly afterwards in July 1885. This line crossed the River Esk on an impressive 13 arch brick viaduct – Larpool Viaduct – immediately south of Airy Hill so that the railway reached the north bank of the river at such a height that it could join the WR&MUR line about half way on its descent from West Cliff station. Inconveniently this meant that any train to and from Scarborough using the main terminal station in Whitby, had to stop in West Cliff station first to change direction.

Whitby viewed from Larpool c.1883, the single track branch promoted by the Whitby, Redcar & Middlesbrough Union Railway (WR&MUR) seen still under construction on the far left, climbing away above the W&PR double tracks. (Author's collection)

Larpool Viaduct carried the line between Scarborough and Prospect Hill Junction, Whitby, across the River Esk just south of the town. The 915ft (279m) long viaduct, 120ft (37m) at its highest point, was built as a vital part of the Scarborough & Whitby Railway between 1882 and 1884, the company retaining its independence until absorbed by the NER in 1898. The tracks of the W&PR can been seen passing underneath nearest the river, with the single line of the WR&MUR a little higher, curving sharply away to Prospect Hill and Whitby West Cliff station. (J. Chesney via R. Carpenter)

All the lines mentioned so far were not just built for the benefit of passengers but were well used by mineral and freight trains. In all parts of the country during the nineteenth century and well into the twentieth, a huge quantity and variety of items were moved by rail, as was an almost incalculable tonnage of coal of all grades used to run stationary and locomotive steam engines, feed the boilers of boats and ships and to be burnt in countless hearths heating homes, schools, shops and all sorts of other premises.

Also vital to the Victoria economy was the manufacture of iron and steel. In this the W&PR played its part by initially providing an outlet for locally produced raw materials and then later as a means of distributing semi-finished goods. Grosmont owed much

of its development as a town to its lime kilns and the mining of iron ore. There were a number of mines immediately north-east of the town connected to the railway, tens of thousands of tons of iron ore extracted during the nineteenth century finding its way to furnaces in the north-east.

With the seemingly endless demand for cast-iron products during the nineteenth century, where raw materials were close at hand it was not unusual for small companies to invest in smelting their own iron, the main ingredients being iron ore, limestone and coke. Two such ironworks were established with sidings connected to the W&PR, the first built by the Whitby

A view looking due west down Front Street, Grosmont in the 1920s. The station buildings are visible above the delivery lorry, and behind that is the tall, brick chimney of the 1860s ironworks that provided so much employment in the town until the beginning of the twentieth century. (Commercial postcard, author's collection)

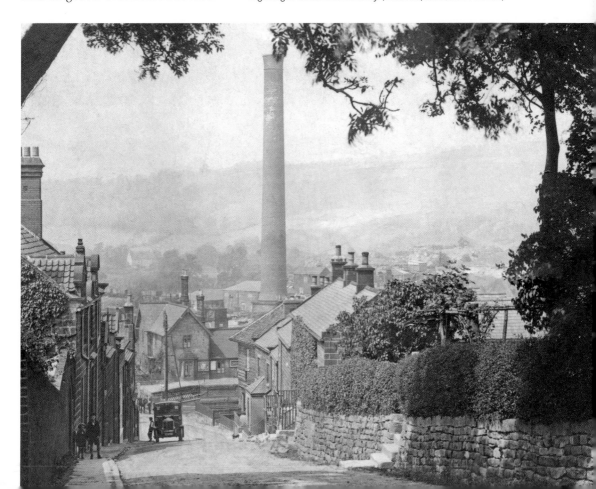

A photograph of NER 0-6-0 No. 659 in fully lined out, dark green livery, taken outside Whitby engine shed in the 1890s. This type of locomotive with a long boiler and oddly spaced, coupled wheels, dated back to an 1866 William Bouch design for the Stockton & Darlington Railway. A number of these old-fashioned locomotives finished their working lives at Whitby and Malton sheds. (Ken Nunn col/The Locomotive Club of Great Britain)

Iron Company Ltd at Beck Hole in 1857. Two blast furnaces for producing pig-iron from ore mined on site were erected, and in 1860 the firm cast its first iron products. Unfortunately problems forced the works to close after only a few years although mining continued a little longer.

More successful was the ironworks set up by Charles and Thomas Bagnall in 1862 to the north-west of the recently opened new railway junction at Grosmont. Two state-of-the-art blast furnaces were 'blown-in' the following year and two of the existing iron ore mines were taken over by the company.

The ironworks soon became the major employer in the town, with 500 people working there. In 1876 a third blast furnace was brought into use, the works remaining in production until 1891. For many years after that, the by-product slag was reprocessed and taken away from the site by rail, the Balcony Slag Works still being recorded in the 1956 edition of the Railway Clearing House Book of Stations.

The industry with a connection to the railway that boasted the longest life at Grosmont in its original form, however, was the brickworks established in 1870 on the opposite side of the line to the ironworks. As well as for numerous domestic buildings its hard, dark red bricks were used for some prestigious buildings such as the Roman

Catholic church of St Joseph, West Hartlepool, opened in 1895. Investment after the First World War led to the commissioning of a new Hoffman kiln in 1923, and the works remained in production until 1957.

Elsewhere on the line, building stone continued to be quarried at Lease Rigg, and the hard, dark coloured Whinstone that was used as an aggregate in road construction was quarried and mined around Goathland. These raw materials were sent out of the area by rail. The inclined plane on which the loaded narrow gauge wagons descended to sidings immediately to the east of Goathland Station, remained a prominent feature until mining ended there after the Second World War.

The limestone quarries just north of Pickering station and served by a siding running north-west behind New Bridge signalbox, remained in production until 1966.

There is little doubt the railways of Great Britain reached their zenith in the twenty years leading up to the First World War. It is fortunate that in this period hundreds of photographs were taken of railway subjects and many turned into picture postcards. Enlargements from a few are used in this book. Although these images appear to

By the end of the nineteenth century, the railways of Great Britain were the most efficient and quickest way of travelling around the country. Here, a three coach train steams purposefully away from Pickering bound for Whitby. In 1899, the early morning Mail Train would have taken just forty-nine minutes to complete that journey, an ordinary passenger a round hour. (S. Smith commercial postcard, author's collection)

show a respectable and well-managed environment, the Edwardian era and the conflict that followed marked a distinct watershed in the social and economic life of the country. There were times when the Government, industrialists and managers worried about revolution amongst workers who were increasingly prepared to strike for better pay and conditions. Yet during Edwardian summers, thousands of workers, happily and peacefully flocked to the seaside and other 'picturesque' destinations during official works holidays. Railway managers and their workforce not on holiday exploited this demand and rose to the considerable challenges of organising and operating the services.

Scarborough and Whitby had already become firmly established by the end of the nineteenth century as popular holiday destinations for both local and long distance travellers. The Great Northern Railway (GNR), for example, had been running regular through

A detail from another Edwardian photograph that was turned into a postcard. It was taken just north of Pickering. The locomotive at the front is a NER Class 38 4-4-0, built to the designs of Alexander McDonnell, company Locomotive Superintendent for a very short period between November 1882 and September 1884. Behind, is a Bogie Tank Passenger (BTP) 0-4-4T designed in 1873 by McDonnell's predecessor, Edward Fletcher, for working such branch lines as that between Rillington Junction, Pickering and Whitby. (Commercial postcard, author's collection)

The south end of Whitby station at the beginning of the twentieth century. The large roof of the goods shed can be seen on the left, with three, four-wheeled passenger carriages in front. Immediately above the signals the remains of the thirteenth century Whitby Benedictine Abbey can be seen on the skyline. (Pat Rutherford)

Another veteran NER 0-6-0, this time photographed at Malton in 1904, where locomotives were shedded for working over the Rillington Junction to Whitby route. This particular engine continued in service until 1909. (Ken Nunn col/The Locomotive Club of Great Britain)

Beckhole.   Auto-Car.   Station

Staff and children pose proudly next to an 'Autocar' at Beck Hole halt a few years before the outbreak of the First World War. (Author's collection)

carriages during the summer months from London Kings Cross since the end of the 1880s. Within a few years of the Great Central Railway (GCR) opening its 'London Extension' from just north of Nottingham to London Marylebone in 1899, it had put on a train to and from Scarborough as an extension of its restaurant car service between Southampton and York. As well as these services, the NER also laid on many holiday excursions from all parts of its own network of lines in Yorkshire and the north-east. In addition, during the summer of 1905, it introduced 'Autocars' between Whitby and Goathland for

day-trippers, augmented three years later using the same type of trains by services to and from a new wooden platform at Beck Hole on the original course of the W&PR. Beck Hole had long been a romantic holiday destination for the more adventurous in the area. The 'Autocars' consisted of a steam locomotive permanently attached to one or a pair of carriages, and because the train could be driven from either the engine or the rear carriage, the former did not have to be 'run around' its train at the end of each journey.

As soon as war was declared in 1914 these services and all excursions were withdrawn, to make way for trains that carried away thousands of naive volunteers as though they were going on just another form of excursion, except not to the British seaside, but to the battlefields of France. Ironically the bombardment by the German Navy of Scarborough, Whitby and Hartlepool on 16 December 1914, in which 137 people died and nearly 600 were injured, both encouraged further recruitment – 'Remember Scarborough!' becoming the new slogan – and brought home the realities of warfare to ordinary people. Under Government control from the very start of the conflict, the railways curtailed many other services so they could move

vast quantities of armaments and men. As the war dragged on, further cuts were made with many stations forced to close in 1916 and 1917, and many miles of track taken up ostensibly for use in France. One of the locations where this occurred was between Pickering and Levisham, where the up (south-bound) line was recovered and single line working instigated between New Bridge and Levisham signalboxes.

A mixed goods train approaching Levisham station from the south just before the First World War, when the line between there and Pickering was still double track. The third, fourth, fifth and sixth vehicles in the train were cattle wagons, the lime used for disinfecting them clearly visible on the lower parts of their bodies. (S. Smith commercial postcard, author's collection)

Decline
to Closure

By the end of the First World War, the great age of railways in Britain had passed. The story of many lines post-1918, including the route through the North Yorkshire Moors, is one of struggle exacerbated by a world-wide recession. Although the transporting of both passengers and freight over long distances remained firmly under the control of the railways, motor lorries siphoned off much local traffic, and by the start of the Second World War there were many more families who owned cars. By the 1930s, the railways to and from Whitby were only really busy during the summer months when hundreds of holiday-makers used ordinary services or took advantage of the many special excursions. During the winter months, far fewer people travelled by train. Industries along the line did not completely abandon the railway and there was even an interesting additional traffic flow created when in 1919 the Pickering Sand Co. invested in a 2.5mile (4km) long narrow gauge railway that followed Gundale Beck to connect its quarries near Saintoft Grange to the sidings at New Bridge, Pickering. The firm and the railway survived the Second World War, remaining in use until 1961.

But despite this specific resurgence, and temporary boosts in traffic due to forestry activity and its need to move timber, retaining business for the railway through the North Yorkshire Moors – both goods and passenger – became increasingly difficult between the two world wars and immediately after 1945.

The London &
North Eastern Railway

In 1923, all the country's railways, with the inevitable few exceptions, were grouped into four new organisations – the NER being absorbed into the London & North Eastern Railway (LNER). The line between Whitby and Rillington Junction then became an even smaller part of a larger undertaking. Double track was never reinstated between Pickering and Levisham as the LNER considered the expenditure was not warranted. Between Whitby and Pickering in the winter months there were just five passenger trains during the week (working through to Malton), a journey stopping at all stations taking a few minutes under the hour. Sunday trains did not reappear in the timetable until the mid 1930s by which time Rillington Junction station had closed to passengers (in September 1930).

One and a half miles (2.5 kilometres) north-east of Goathland station, high up on the Whinstone Ridge on Sleights Moor, this road sign from the horse-drawn age was being seen by an increasing number of motor vehicles when this photograph was taken in the 1920s.
(Commercial postcard, author's collection)

Ten years after the Grouping of the railways, and the majority of locomotives seen at Whitby were former North Eastern Railway (NER) designs. In this 1934 photograph, London & North Eastern Railway (LNER) Class A6 4-6-2T No. 693 dominates the scene on the right, overshadowing its older stable mate, 2-4-2T LNER Class F8 No. 1581, designed in 1885 by T.W. Worsdell. The A6 class was designed by his brother, Wilson Worsdell, especially for working the Whitby to Scarborough line, and ten were constructed between 1907 and 1908. (T.E. Rounthwaite)

The south end of Pickering station on a bright summer morning in the 1920s. The crossing gates on Bridge Street are closed and the train is ready to pull away to Rillington Junction and Malton. The tracks on the left lead to the goods yard. (S. Smith commercial postcard, author's collection)

Former Hull & Barnsley Railway (H&BR) 0-6-0 LNER Class J23 No. 2453 hurries through Goathland station in June 1934 with a south-bound freight train, crossing the Eller Beck in the foreground. This J23 was one of a number of the class shedded at Whitby and Malton for working between the two places. The last two of the class were withdrawn from service at Whitby in 1938. (R. Carpenter collection)

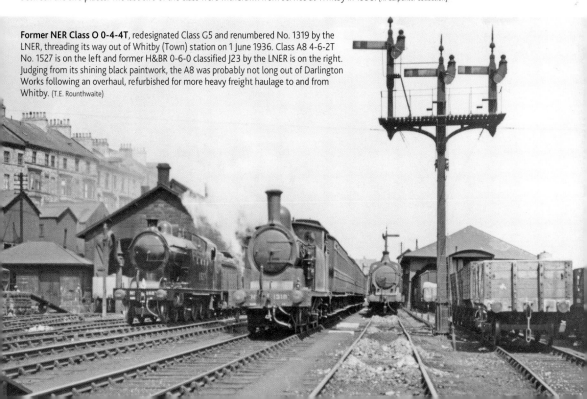

Former NER Class O 0-4-4T, redesignated Class G5 and renumbered No. 1319 by the LNER, threading its way out of Whitby (Town) station on 1 June 1936. Class A8 4-6-2T No. 1527 is on the left and former H&BR 0-6-0 classified J23 by the LNER is on the right. Judging from its shining black paintwork, the A8 was probably not long out of Darlington Works following an overhaul, refurbished for more heavy freight haulage to and from Whitby. (T.E. Rounthwaite)

Another Class G5, this time no. 1886 hauling the 12.10pm departure from Whitby and approaching Grosmont in 1938. Despite the date, all the railway hardware that can be seen was of NER vintage: the engine, carriages, track and telegraph pole. (Real Photos)

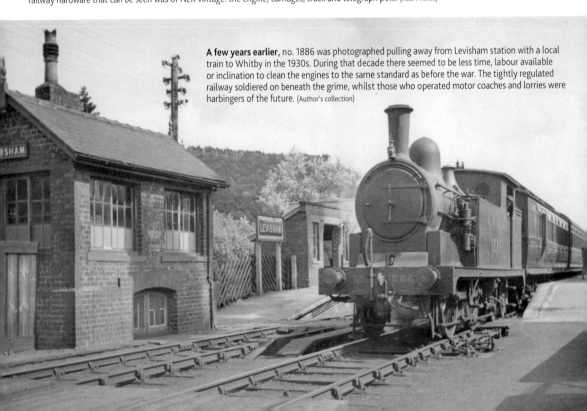

A few years earlier, no. 1886 was photographed pulling away from Levisham station with a local train to Whitby in the 1930s. During that decade there seemed to be less time, labour available or inclination to clean the engines to the same standard as before the war. The tightly regulated railway soldiered on beneath the grime, whilst those who operated motor coaches and lorries were harbingers of the future. (Author's collection)

The look and operation of Goathland station changed little after the First World War. As can be seen in this late 1930s photograph, goods trains were still well loaded, like this one hauled by a 0-6-0 LNER Class J24 and needing banking assistance on the climb from Grosmont. At the station itself, economies meant the station master was shared with Levisham, but there was still investment in local industries using the railway, as illustrated by the construction to the right of a new weighbridge office built by the LNER for the Goathland Whinstone Quarries under an agreement of June 1939. (Author's collection)

LNER tickets. (P. Waller collection)

As stated earlier, it was in the summer months when the branches to Whitby and the coast earned their money. Between Malton and Whitby, two extra weekday trains with four extras on Saturdays were added to the summer timetables. In addition, the Whitby–Goathland 'Autocar' services resumed after the war, replaced from 1932 by single carriage steam railcars built by the Sentinel Waggon Works in Shrewsbury. Each of these vehicles was given a name, many previously carried by early nineteenth century stage coaches, a practice that also recalled the earliest days on the W&PR when the horse-drawn railway coaches were named. The

Sentinels' distinctive livery of green and cream also echoed the coaching era and made them stand out against the standard teak and dark brown colouring of ordinary LNER carriages. They proved popular for both operators and passengers, and they became a familiar sight on many LNER branch lines throughout the 1930s.

The Sentinels' cheerful colour arrangement was soon applied to new excursion stock built by the LNER from 1933. The company was keen to maintain its hold on long distant summer excursions, laying on services that carried as many passengers as possible at the cheapest fares, as well prestigious ones such as the 'Northern Belle', running from Kings Cross and routed through the North Yorkshire Moors as part of a luxury 'scenic cruise' around the country. Another ploy by the LNER (and other railway companies) trying to boost their income, was the hiring

Six-cylinder Sentinel railcar No. 248, *Tantivy* being topped up with coal at Whitby in September 1938. It had a very short working life, being built at the very end of 1932 at the Sentinel Waggon Works in Shrewsbury then withdrawn immediately on the outbreak of the Second World War. Tantivy was a word describing rapid movement and was applied to a number of horse-drawn stage coaches in the previous century. In the 1830s, when travelling behind a steam engine offered faster journeys than by road, it is said stage coach drivers sang: 'Let the steam pot hiss till it's hot, Give me the speed of the Tantivy Trot.' (W. Potter)

Railcars, some steam and others petrol driven, were intended to improve the image of railway travel in the 1930s and cut down on operating costs. These vehicles were deliberately given colourful cream and light green liveries to set them apart from ordinary railway carriages and to make them as eye-catching as motor buses. Number 237 *Rodney*, seen here, was one of twenty, two-cylinder Sentinel steam railcars built in 1928 and used initially on Forge Valley services to and from Pickering. (Author's collection)

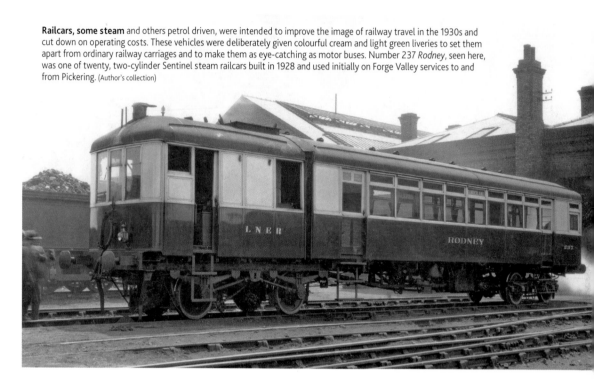

Railcar No. 2257 *Defiance* was one of twenty-eight vehicles built by Sentinel's of Shrewsbury in 1929. It was photographed with another unidentified example at Whitby, probably at the end of the 1930s. It was withdrawn at the end of the Second World War. *Defiance* was another name taken from old stage coach services, two examples once operating around Exeter, and between Glasgow and Aberdeen. (Author's collection)

Former NER 4-6-2T, LNER Class A6 No. 692 at Whitby in October 1938, its black bulk contrasting with the up-to-date motor bus on the road immediately behind. (W. Potter)

One of the innovations aimed at persuading people back to the railway in the 1930s was the fitting out of old passenger carriages as camping coaches. These were placed in sidings at a number of stations in Yorkshire, including Goathland. This snap-shot of that station sometime before the Second World War, was undoubtedly taken by the family staying in the camping coach there. The carriage roof can just be seen immediately to the right of the woman in the fashionable hat. (Author's collection)

out of camping coaches converted from redundant stock. These were parked in little used sidings at Levisham and Goathland stations as well as at other stations on neighbouring lines.

In the last years of the 1930s the country-wide economic depression was easing, but it was becoming increasingly obvious that another war was almost inevitable, and the Government was making preparations. When war with Germany was declared in 1939, the railways were immediately requisitioned and train services all over the country were severely reduced. Between Whitby and Malton the weekday timetable was reduced to just four trains each way. Whitby once again became a German target but from the air rather than the sea. One of the first enemy bombers to be shot down over the country crashed just outside the town, and in another raid a year later, the south end of the goods shed was destroyed and track uprooted. The station house at Grosmont also suffered minor damage in a later attack.

British Railways

For the first few years after the war, apart from the challenges for returning service personnel of settling back into civilian life and with rationing still in force, in locations such as the North Yorkshire Moors very little appeared to change. Nevertheless, there was an optimism that life should and would be better than in pre-war days. The obvious indicator of this perception was the landslide victory achieved by the Labour Party in the 1945 General Election. Churchill was almost universally admired for steering the country through its worst crisis for centuries, but the people wanted their say in its future, and many felt it was socialism that was going to deliver true change and not a Tory stalwart. As promised, the Labour Party nationalised the country's staple industries of coal mining and steel production; nationalised the water, gas

The LNER's October 1947 timetable as published in Bradshaw's Guide. (Author's collection)

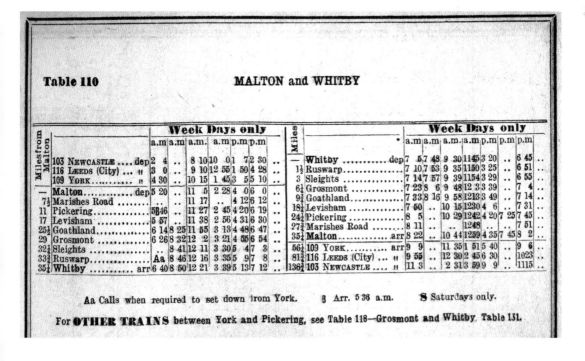

and electricity supply industries; and nationalised road haulage, waterways and the railways. In 1948, British Railways came into existence, which reduced the Whitby to Pickering line to an even smaller cog in a huge and increasingly unwieldy machine.

The people's love of the socialist experiment, however, did not last long, and in 1951 a Conservative Government was returned to power. That administration delivered road haulage back into the hands of hundreds of ambitious private owners, and as bus services expanded and car ownership increased, British Railways – still firmly in public ownership – was forced to implement the economies that the pre-

War companies knew were inevitable but had not been prepared to make. The cuts had already started before the General Election, passenger trains having stopped running over the Forge Valley Line between Pickering and Seamer from 4 June 1950. On 18 September 1951, barely a month after Churchill was returned to power, the last train on the branch to Beck Hole ran, after the former mining settlement of Esk Valley 1 mile (1.6km) south of Grosmont, previously only connected to the outside world by this line, was provided with a new road by North Riding County Council. Then from 1 February 1953 it was no longer possible to travel as a passenger by train between Pickering and Gilling via Kirby Moorside. In June the following year, passenger services between Whitby and Middlesbrough via Grosmont were modified, trains no longer running to Picton but reversing at Battersby Junction.

Putting on a show as it entered Goathland station from the north on 15 September 1950 with a long goods train, over two and a half years after nationalisation, this Class J24 0-6-0 No. 5644 was still in its LNER livery – hidden under the grime. It had, however, been fitted with a new cast shed plate – 50F – indicating that it was officially allocated to Malton motive power depot (MPD), of which Pickering was a sub-shed. It was withdrawn the year after this photograph was taken. (Author's collection)

Former LNER 4-4-0 Class D49, No. 62731 *Selkirkshire,* in the first manifestation of the new nationalised railway's livery, leaving Levisham for Pickering and Malton. The train was made up of former NER carriages. (Cecil Ord collection)

A Malton–Whitby service pulling away from Levisham station in the early 1950s behind former NER 0-4-4T, LNER Class G5 No. 67335. This locomotive was built in 1901 and lasted in service until 1953. (Cecil Ord collection)

There followed a respite of four years, then passenger services were further reduced when at the beginning of May 1958 trains stopped running between Whitby and Loftus, although West Cliff station remained open for trains to and from Scarborough until June 1961.

After that passenger trains travelling between Whitby and Scarborough changed directions at Prospect Hill Junction, Whitby, a process made easier as since 1958 diesel multiple units (DMUs) had been substituted for steam trains on this route. In 1959, DMUs also took over all but two of the five daily trains south of Whitby.

But steam haulage continued for all summer excursion traffic over the line, and through carriages from Kings Cross detached at York for Whitby still had to be attached to other steam worked trains in order to complete their journey. For this brief period in the late 1950s and early 1960s, the old and new ways of operating a railway co-existed.

Then came the Beeching Report of 1963, the result of a clinical analysis of every part of the British Railways network. The simple aim outlined in that report was to make the railways pay their way by accelerating modernisation and cutting away all unprofitable

A few pages from British Railways' 1950 'Holiday Guide' to Eastern England.
(Author's collection)

A poor photograph taken on 31 January 1953, but one that shows the signalbox at Mill Lane, Pickering, where the line from Gilling, Helmsley and Kirkby Moorside came in from the west (right) and the Forge Valley line from Seamer and Thornton Dale joined the Rillington Junction to Whitby route from the east (left). The Forge Valley line had closed to passengers in 1950, with services through Kirkby Moorside ending on 2 February 1953, a few days after this photograph was taken. (Kidderminster Railway Museum 005237)

A summer holiday train from Whitby on the climb through Beck Hole with 4-6-0 Class B1 No. 61086 based at Neville Hill (Leeds) on the front and an unidentified locomotive banking at the rear. As was typical of the mid-1950s period, the engine had not been cleaned externally for many months, and all but two of the carriages of the eight coach train were former LNER teak-bodied examples, probably worse for wear after intensive war-time use. (Cecil Ord)

As local traffic disappeared from branch lines during the 1950s, summer specials between the cities of northern England and the coast became a vital source of revenue for a nationalised railway struggling to balance its books. In this photograph from the late-1950s, 0-4-4T Class G5 No. 67342 pilots 4-6-0 Class B1 around the curves at Goathland Summit with a lengthy Leeds–Whitby train. (Cecil Ord)

Holiday time at Whitby Town station in the mid-1950s. On the right, LNER 4-4-0 Class D49 No. 62731 *Selkirkshire* making another appearance and blowing off fiercely at the head of a train of former LNER teak carriages repainted in British Railways' new crimson lake and cream livery, often referred to as 'blood and custard'. In the centre road is 2-6-4T No. 80117, built at Brighton Works in 1954 and sent to Whitby shed that year. It stayed until 1958. (T.J. Edgington)

Coasting down grade on the last mile towards Grosmont with a local train from Malton, 2-6-4T Class 4P No. 42083 was returning to its home shed at Whitby where it was resident between October 1955 and July 1959. (Cecil Ord)

South-bound mixed goods train behind former NER Class P3 0-6-0, British Railways Class J27 No. 65888 at Darnholm on the climb towards Goathland station in the 1950s. Like the J24, this was a local engine shedded at Malton. The first P3 was turned out of Darlington Works in 1906 and the last of over 100 engines appeared in 1923 after the Grouping. This final example – No. 2392 – was withdrawn in 1967 and acquired by the North Eastern Locomotive Preservation Group (NELPG) nine years later to work on the recently formed North Yorkshire Moors Railway. (Cecil Ord collection)

activities. In North Yorkshire this meant eliminating all the remaining passenger services between Whitby, Scarborough, Middlesbrough and Pickering. The line between Middlesborough and Whitby would be retained for freight traffic as it was the one local line making the smallest loss, according to statistics gathered for the report. The same statistics claimed that the complete closure of the line between Grosmont and Rillington Junction would save almost £50,000 a year.

Beeching's plans were the most controversial in railway history and there was huge opposition to his proposals. Any objections had to be channelled through the regional Transport Users' Consultative Committees (TUCC) that were tasked with considering individual cases of hardship that might be caused by any closures. Public meetings were held in Whitby at the beginning of July 1964 at which it was stressed how important the railway was during bad winters when local roads were impassable and children had to rely on trains to get to and from Whitby schools, and what a detrimental effect withdrawal of passenger trains would have on the town's tourist trade. In August the Yorkshire TUCC made its report having received over 2,000 objections to Beeching's plans.

It seemed a strong case had been made, but the following month the Transport Minister, Ernest Marples, announced that passenger service would only be retained between Whitby and Middlesborough, and that the line south of Grosmont would be scheduled for complete closure.

With the defeat of the Conservative Party in the following month's election and the installation of a Labour administration, hopes were high that the 'Beeching Axe' might be blunted.

Looking in the opposite direction to the photograph at the top of page 51, an evening return seaside special from Whitby has more of a challenge climbing out of Grosmont on the 1 in 49 gradient. Piloting the 4-6-0 Class B1 (the train engine) was 2-6-4T Class 4P No. 42639, and as its shed plate (50F) indicates it was allocated to Malton at the time, the photograph must have been taken sometime between June 1960 and November the following year. (Cecil Ord)

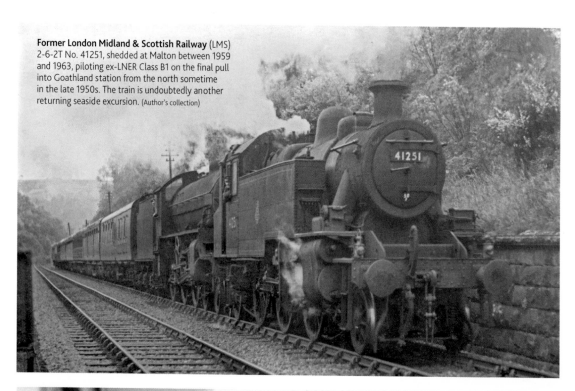

Former London Midland & Scottish Railway (LMS) 2-6-2T No. 41251, shedded at Malton between 1959 and 1963, piloting ex-LNER Class B1 on the final pull into Goathland station from the north sometime in the late 1950s. The train is undoubtedly another returning seaside excursion. (Author's collection)

Swinging southwards through Newton Dale on 11 October 1961. (D. Hardy)

A deserted **Whitby Town station** in the mid-1950s, although there are trains at both number two and three platforms. On the extreme right, part of the stone-built York & North Midland Railway goods shed that was extensively damaged in the Second World War, with the much later brick signalbox attached to its corner. (J.W. Armstrong)

Another former NER 4-6-2T Class A8 No. 69889 waiting at Whitby Town station's Platform 3 on 26 June 1957. The truncated goods shed nestles up against the signalbox. Beyond, the goods yard appears busy alongside a row of carriages parked ready for returning holiday-makers. (Hugh Davies 176a)

The 6.57pm Whitby–Malton service battling up the 1 in 49 gradient between Grosmont and Goathland in the 1950s behind ex-NER 4-6-2T Class A8 No. 69861. The engine had been built at Darlington Works in 1913 and allocated to Whitby shed on two separate occasions in 1950 and 1952. It spent its last days at Malton until withdrawn in June 1960 after a creditable 46 years service. (Cecil Ord collection)

British Railways 2-6-0 Class 3 No. 77012 was an example of one of the smallest 'standard' class of locomotives designed for the nationalised railway. It was photographed at Darnholm hauling a Whitby–York train southwards on 5 September 1958, the cast 50G shed plate attached to its smokebox door indicating that at the time it was allocated to Whitby shed. (Cecil Ord collection)

But closures already agreed were not reversed, despite an ill-judged election campaign statement made by Harold Wilson MP that many took to mean the route through the North Yorkshire Moors would be protected. In the end, the only concession was that track and signalling were to be keep in situ between Grosmont and Goathland in case trains had to be used to carry school children in the winter. No track further south could be removed but other equipment could be recovered.

The last regular passenger trains between Whitby and Malton ran on Saturday 6 March 1965, with the addition of a steam special, 'The Whitby Moors', organised by the Stephenson Locomotive Society and the Manchester Locomotive Society, and run behind two preserved 2-6-0s, *The Great Marquess* and K1 No. 62005. Then as if to justify the retention of track, eight months after British Railways had withdrawn passenger trains on the line, it was called upon to run specials on 29 and 30 November 1965 as the school bus was unable to negotiate the snow between Whitby and Goathland. This gesture, however, was never repeated.

The need to move limestone away from the New Bridge quarry and bring in domestic coal to Pickering kept the line between there and Rillington Junction open for a further seven months until complete closure on 2 July 1966. By then, the Whitby to Pickering line had been in existence for almost exactly 130 years.

British Railways tickets. (P. Waller collection)

The signalman has just handed the Levisham–New Bridge (Pickering) single line token to the crew of Class B1 4-6-0 No. 61062 hauling this south-bound train entering Levisham station on 17 August 1963. It was just five months after publication of the 'Re-Shaping of British Railways' – the Beeching Report – proposing the closure of the whole route between Rillington Junction and Grosmont and the withdrawal of all passenger services to and from Whitby. Levisham station would be one of the casualties. (R.N. Joanes)

Pickering station as it looked at the end of its ownership by British Railways, the last timetabled passenger train running through on 6 March 1965. (D. Lawrence 5672a)

Revival

When the closure plans were announced, there were three good reasons put forward for retaining the line between Grosmont and Pickering. The first was to maintain a public service. The second was as a tourist attraction, a place where you could travel on a steam train. The third was as a way of controlling access to the North York Moors National Park (designated as such in 1952) by persuading visitors out of their cars and into trains. All three arguments were put forward immediately before and then after closure, but it was the second reason that initially triumphed over the others.

Two powerful drivers ensured the North Yorkshire Moors Railway (NYMR) emerged as a tourist attraction. The first was the timing of the closure. There had been widespread dismay at what the Beeching Plan of 1963 had wrought on the national rail network. In very few places had the case for closure of a line or station been successfully challenged. This impotency in the face of officialdom had inspired many to seek to run their own lines, spurred on by the achievement of the Bluebell Railway Preservation Society in 1960, and by the fighting spirit shown by other groups such as the one trying to reopen the Keighley & Worth Valley Railway.

These groups, and others that were emerging, were also symptoms of a wider reaction to the 1960s remodelling of the country's towns and cities and the replacement of Georgian and Victorian architecture with concrete tower blocks, shopping precincts and octopus-like road schemes. For a new generation, post-war modernisation had become tarnished. As the planners continued to pursue the demolish–rebuild happiness dream, there was an increasing number of ordinary people who were prepared to turn up at weekends and get their hands dirty digging out overgrown canals and rescuing all kinds of ordinary, 'working class' things that had been rapidly disappearing over the previous decade. These people were unpaid, it was not their job, they were not museum curators, but they wanted to preserve mills, mangles and milling machines, and perhaps the most emotive of all Victorian engineering achievements that were going to the scrap yards – steam locomotives.

The elimination of steam engines from British Railways in 1968 and the subsequent ban of running any but the *Flying Scotsman* on the national network after that date further encouraged the preservationists. If steam engines were to be seen, heard and smelt, then it had to be on private lines run by volunteers.

All this desire to preserve, however, would have borne different fruit if the NYMR had not passed through such inspiring scenery, and this was undoubtedly the second most important reason for the success of this railway as a tourist attraction. It is one of those ironies not always voiced, that although steam locomotives were products of an industrialised nation, in which the majority of the population lived and worked in towns and cities, most people go to visit them and travel behind them because they run in the countryside.

The First 25 Years (1967–1993)

British Railways had been obliged to leave the track *in situ* between Grosmont

Built in 1955, saddle tank 0-4-0 *Mirvale* was the first steam locomotive to be operated on the North Yorkshire Moors Railway (NYMR) by the new preservation society, at the beginning of 1969. The engine was named after the firm it originally worked for – Mirvale Chemicals in Mirfield. It is seen here at Goathland station on Easter Monday, 12 April 1971, only sixteen days after the North Yorkshire Moors Historical Railway Trust had been created. (Tony Wickens/Online Transport Archive/2604)

and Rillington Junction for two years after closure. As the expiry of this embargo approached, efforts to acquire the section of line between Grosmont and Pickering rested with the North Yorkshire Moors Railway Preservation Society (NYMRPS), formed in November 1967. With a price tag of £120,000 beyond the reach of the new group, the more realistic target became the purchase of all the trackbed, but only a single line of rails for 5.5 miles (8.85km) from Grosmont

Ticket No. 1051 issued by the NYMR at Goathland station on 27 June 1970 for two shillings (10p). (Author's collection)

Ticket No. 101, one of those issued on 27 June 1970 to members of the NYMR for travel between Grosmont and Ellerbeck, three years before the line was reopened through to Pickering. (Author's collection)

Ellerbeck was remote enough, and the disruption caused by creating and then operating a new terminus for the railway there encouraged the Parks Committee and North Riding Council to offer to purchase for the NYMRPC a single track southwards from there to Pickering, thus creating an eighteen mile long preserved railway. In 1969, no preservation society anywhere in the country was operating more than a few miles of single track, but the society was prepared to rise to the challenge.

Grosmont became the centre of activities, with volunteers operating small tank steam locomotives at weekends and Bank Holidays to raise much needed funds. In June 1970 the North Eastern Locomotive Preservation Group's (NELPG) 1918-built NER Class T2 0-8-0, along with Lambton Tank 0-6-2T No. 29 built in 1904, were delivered to the railway. Two months later the latter's sister No. 5 arrived, to be joined in October the following year by the NELPG's 1923-built NER P3 Class 0-6-0. At the very end of that year, the North York Moors Historical Railway Trust (NYMHRT) was created to succeed the NYMRPS, becoming the first registered charity to operate a preserved railway. Paid staff were recruited to join the volunteers, the Light Railway Order for operating trains on the line was transferred from British Rail to the preservationists, and on 1 May 1973, the Duchess of Kent officially opened the North Yorkshire Moors Railway (NYMR). Steam trains for the paying public were then run between Grosmont and Goathland, with a diesel multiple unit (DMU) service to and from Levisham and the outskirts of Pickering.

The fact that trains were not able to use Pickering station at the time indicates that in the late 1960s and early 1970s not everyone was supportive of enthusiastic amateurs running railways.

southwards through Goathland to the summit of the line near Ellerbeck (where the line came closest to the A169). The hope was to extend as future fundraising allowed. Membership of the society increased steadily, and by May 1969 it was able to pay British Railways a 10% deposit on the £42,500 asking price. If they had been unsure of the success of the society before, this event demonstrated to the North York Moors National Parks management that trains would soon be running into the heart of the Park and, rather than reduce the number of cars on local roads, it had the potential to encourage more.

Lined up in the down Platform 2 at Grosmont station on 20 May 1972 are *Mirvale* and Lambton Tank 0-6-2T, No. 29, the latter having been bought by NYMR and North Eastern Locomotive Preservation Group (NELPG) members in 1970. This engine was built in 1904 by Kitson & Co. of Leeds for working on the Lambton Colliery railway system. (Author's collection)

Brought to the NYMR in 1969, 0-6-0ST *Salmon* was built by Andrew Barclay & Sons of Kilmarnock in 1942 to work at Stewarts & Lloyds ironstone quarries in Lincolnshire. It was named after HMS Salmon, a British submarine sunk in 1940. Mirvale and Salmon were in steam at most open days, keeping the public interested and involved until a full passenger service could be operated. In this undated photograph, Salmon pulls an engineering train over the level crossing at Grosmont sometime between 1969 and 1971. (Author's collection)

In this photograph taken at Darnholm on 12 April 1971, Lambton Tank No. 5 is seen climbing the 1 in 49 towards Goathland only eight months after it had arrived on the NYMR. It was constructed by Robert Stephenson & Co. at Darlington in 1909 for use at Lambton Colliery, County Durham. Following a number of mergers with other collieries, by 1924 the Lambton Colliery had expanded its name to Lambton, Hetton & Joicey Collieries, explaining why 0-6-2T No. 5 and 0-6-2T No. 29 have been outshopped at various times in a livery with the initials of this post-1924 company. (Tony Wickens/Online Transport Archive /2609)

Only a month after the NYMR's service south of Goathland had begun, the diesel multiple unit (DMU) hired from British Rail stands at the temporary platform just north of Pickering on 28 May 1973. (Tony Wickens/Online Transport Archive /2604)

Front cover of the booklet issued to commemorate the opening of the NYMR by HRH The Duchess of Kent on 1 May 1973.
(Author's collection)

Pottering about at Goathland in either the summer of 1972 or 1973, is 0-4-0ST No. 15 *Eustace Forth,* which had arrived on the railway in June 1972 and stayed until January 1978. It had been built in 1942 by Robert Stephenson and Hawthorns (a 1937 amalgamation of Robert Stephenson & Co. of Darlington and Hawthorn Leslie & Co. of Newcastle-upon-Tyne), and had been working before preservation at Dunston Power Station.
(Stephenson Locomotive Society)

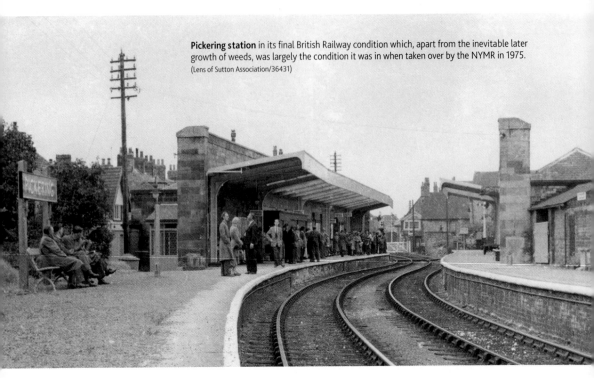

Pickering station in its final British Railway condition which, apart from the inevitable later growth of weeds, was largely the condition it was in when taken over by the NYMR in 1975. (Lens of Sutton Association/36431)

With the line through the town closed, Pickering Urban District Council had plans to modify the town's road layout by eliminating the level crossings on Bridge Street and Hungate and demolishing the station so that the site could be used for a supermarket and car park. The Council's application to compulsorily purchase the station site provoked a public enquiry at which Council representatives did not help their cause by describing the NYMR as '… a plaything for the affluent society.' A petition in favour of retaining the station was signed by 1,400 local residents with only 33 in opposition, and with over 75,000 tickets sold since passenger services restarted, the sensible outcome was that Pickering station should remain for the use of NYMR's trains.

Another Light Railway Order was granted and the station came back into use on 24 May 1975. With the public enquiry out of the way, Pickering Urban District Council wasted no time in demolishing the goods shed and coal drops between Bridge Street and Hungate, driving through a new road on the former track bed and laying out a public car park between those two roads.

For the new NYMR, the reverberations of the decision to operate the longest preserved railway in the country continued throughout that decade. The first chairman of the Trust, Richard Rowntree, expressed misgivings about the move away from a 'little' line that he believed could be run with volunteers, to one that might be considered as part of a strategy by others to keep road traffic out of a national park and would need far more resourcing than volunteers could muster. His opinion was supported, when in 1974 it was revealed that because British Rail were not able to provide second-hand track to repair and renew the line between Ellerbeck and Pickering at the £6,000 it had quoted, the NYMR had been obliged to spend in excess of

Former NER Class P3 0-6-0 No. 2392 inside the partly completed new locomotive shed south of Grosmont Tunnel in March 1973. After heading the NYMR re-opening train from Whitby on 1 May that year it went on to share the burden of hauling passenger services between Grosmont and Goathland with Lambton Tank No. 29, its partner in that re-opening train. The P3 was not worked as hard again until the early 1990s. (Author's collection)

£21,000 on renewals. The North York Moors National Park Committee was quickly made aware of this and agreed to inject £20,000 into track upgrading. In April 1981, when the single platform Newton Dale Halt was opened between Levisham and Goathland, it was primarily of benefit to those using the National Park rather than meeting any needs the NYMR might have had in that remote spot.

Throughout the 1970s, the NYMR attracted more and more volunteers, locomotives and rolling stock as passenger numbers also increased year on year. In 1977, some 250,000 passengers travelled on the line, and by the end of the 1981 season, that figure had risen to 320,000. (It is interesting to record that in that year, the annual wages bill of permanent staff employed by the railway amounted to £120,000, the same figure that British Rail had been asking for the purchase of the land and track between Grosmont and Pickering back in 1967.) The NYMR had become the most popular heritage railway in the country.

But as with all emerging heritage railways, income from passengers never covered operating costs, and so bank loans kept the trains running in those early years. Capital expenditure was also severely restricted by what could be raised from special appeals, and whereas other preserved lines constituted as limited companies, or with such supporting organisations, began to raise capital by share issues during this period, the NYMR was constrained by being a registered charity with no trading arm. In 1984/5, the Trust looked on enviously at the Severn Valley Railway (SVR) as it extended to Kidderminster and

Former NER Class T2 0-8-0 No. 2238 with a full head of steam outside 'Tunnel Cottages', Grosmont on 9 October 1976. The whole scene gives a good impression of the early years of the NYMR when enthusiasm and hard physical work were the main ingredients for keeping the trains running. Until 1989 the cottages provided accommodation for volunteers. (Author's collection)

raised funds at such a rate that it was immediately able to construct a new, large brick terminal station based on authentic Great Western Railway architecture, and have enough left over to finance the building of a brand new sixty-seven lever signalbox with all the associated signalling (completed in 1987).

In 1986, the first ideas for a lavish revamp of Whitby station that would rival the Kidderminster creation were aired in 'Moors Line' (No. 74) – the magazine of the North York Moors Historical Railway Trust. This started the discussions as to whether the NYMR would ever be able to fund such a project if it could not resort to issuing shares. With the

inevitable answer being no, it was no surprise that at the last Council meeting of 1987, the Chairman of the NYMHRT proposed a share issue. This in turn led to a study into the benefits or otherwise of setting up a plc, the interim report being submitted at the end of 1989. Official blessing to such a move was ratified by the NYMHRT on 7 July 1990, leading to the immediate formation of the North Yorkshire Moors Railway Enterprise plc (NYMRE plc).

The first meeting of the new organisation was held twelve days later and then on 8 August a share issue was launched at Grosmont with the National Railway Museum's replica *Rocket* in attendance. The aim was to raise £500,000 for a portfolio of projects ranging from improving the motive power depot (MPD) at Grosmont to extending the platforms at Pickering. By October

£150,000 had been subscribed and when the issue was closed at the end of 1991, the total stood at £245,000.

Unfortunately, that success was soon overshadowed by dissent amongst the 'rank and file' of the railway, concerned about increased commercialism and conflicting priorities. A few unpleasant years followed in which disputes made headlines outside the railway, consultants were brought in, there were resignations and the roles of the new plc and the existing NYMHRT were reappraised.

What helped restore a balance in the railway's affairs were the challenges of a national recession, and the phenomenal popularity of a new television series - 'Heartbeat' – featuring many NYMR locations. Passenger numbers were quickly restored to those of the 1980s boom years and most people associated with the railway found they had a common purpose once again.

Of crucial importance to the survival of the NYMR for the next twenty-five years, as with all heritage railways, was compromise. There have been, and will probably continue to be, tensions between preservation and commercialism, and preservation and operation. The aims and priorities of one group of railway enthusiasts will be different to those of another and there will also be tensions in relation to how operations are carried out and provided for the paying customer. The passage of time also effects how decisions are viewed and the following selective examples will illustrate some of those tensions.

Motive Power

For most of its existence, the NYMR has operated but not owned locomotives. From the beginning, owners of engines were attracted to the line because their machines could be worked hard over a long challenging section of line including a gradient of 1 in 49. To manage their use, the NYMR set up

two forms of locomotive agreement: a service agreement whereby the NYMR maintained, repaired and overhauled the engines using its own staff and resources; and a mileage or historic locomotive agreement in which the owners undertook their own maintenance, repair etc using their own volunteers. Since 1969 those two agreements have been revised on a number of occasions when either the NYMR or the locomotive owners have felt they were not getting value for money. When the line opened in 1973, steam

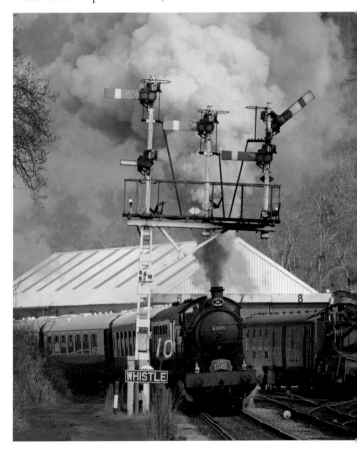

Sporting its former British Railways livery and number, 0-8-0 Class Q6 No. 63395 pulls away purposely from Grosmont on 3 April 2016 with a special birthday party train. The engine was built at Darlington in 1918 by the NER as No. 2238, a member of the large class of T2 locomotives. It was purchased by NELPG in 1968, restored, and ran its first trains on the NYMR in 1970. When this photograph was taken, it had been in preservation for 48 years (1968–2016) only one year less than the time it had spent working, firstly for the NER, then the LNER and finally British Railways (1918–1967). (Author)

Ex-LNER Class A4 No. 60007 *Sir Nigel Gresley* approaching Goathland Summit on 6 October 2013 with a south-bound train. The locomotive was built at Doncaster in 1937 and named after its illustrious designer. With the end of steam traction on British Railways rapidly approaching, a group was set up in 1964 specifically to preserve the engine once it was declared redundant. This happened in 1966 and the locomotive passed into the care of the A4 Preservation Society. The locomotive first came to the NYMR in 1999, after which it became an important visitor attraction for the railway. (Author)

Shortly after another major overhaul, Lambton Tank No. 29 waits to depart from Goathland station on 12 May 2013 with an ex-Great Northern Railway saloon built in 1909. Of all the industrial locomotives that worked on the NYMR during the 1970s it was only this engine and No. 5 that stayed, continuing to perform into the twenty-first century, working alongside more powerful main line locomotives, both resident on the line and visiting from other heritage railways. (Author)

A view from above the tunnels at Grosmont in April 1973. Class P3 0-6-0 No. 2392 stands on the Y&NMR bridge over the River Murk Esk. It was the operation of this engine, alongside former NER 0-8-0 Class T2 No. 2238 (63395), the two Lambton Tanks and LMS 'Black Five' 4-6-0 No. 45428 from 1974, that very quickly propelled the NYMR into the premier league of heritage railways. (Author's collection)

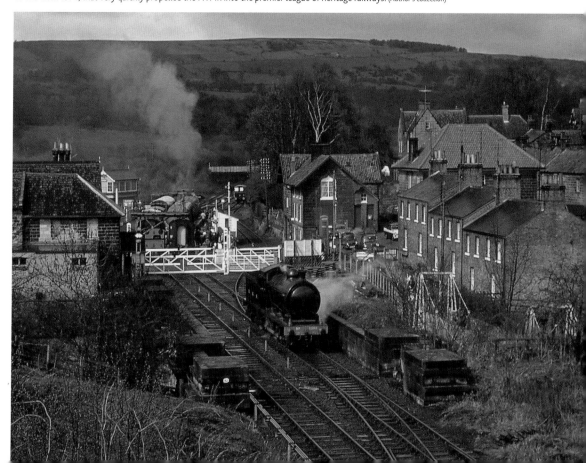

British Railways Class 24 No. D5032, built in 1959 and saved from the scrap yard in 1976 for use on the NYMR. Photographed leaving Grosmont Tunnel on 11 April 2010. (Author)

this title reinforced the view of the then chairman that this section of line was really being operated, unofficially, on behalf of the North York Moors National Park Committee. When it was suggested steam locomotives should replace the DMUs, controversy was stirred by the assertion they would have to be altered to burn oil instead of coal to eliminate the danger of sparks setting fires in Newton Dale. The conversions never took place, and in 1976 the NYMR proudly announced it was to run coal-fired, steam locomotives working over the whole route between Grosmont and Pickering every Sunday from 11 July for eight Sundays, plus Bank Holiday Mondays (19 April and 30 August), with the addition of eight special charter trains. Unfortunately, that summer turned out to be one of the driest on record, and services through the National Park had to be hauled by the increasing number of main line diesels taking up residence at Grosmont.

The most iconic of those diesels were two British Railways Class 55 engines – *Alycidon* and *Royal Highland Fusilier*, members of a fleet of twenty-two locomotives used to operate the principal services over the East Coast main line between 1961 and 1981. In August 1982, the Deltic Preservation Society (DPS) chose to set up its base at the railway with these two machines. Their use, with the other diesels, to haul passenger trains, however, divided opinion amongst both enthusiasts and visitors. In 1985, DMU services on the line ended, and in 1986 more trains were timetabled for steam haulage, 'Moors Line' (No. 86) reporting that the first train out of Pickering was poorly patronised because it was diesel hauled, passengers preferring to wait to ride on a steam train.

In May 1987 *Royal Highland Fusilier* left for the Midland Railway Trust in Derbyshire because the NYMR had been unable to provide undercover accommodation promised to the DPS at

locomotives were used only to haul trains between Grosmont and Goathland. Between there and Pickering, DMUs were purchased by the NYMR to operate a shuttle service. In that year, these were out-shopped in a new corporate livery of green and cream with a painted headboard reading 'The National Park Scenic Cruise'. Perhaps unintentionally,

New Bridge for storage and maintenance. For the 1989 season, the NYMR introduced an almost all-steam timetable with only occasional 'diesel days', following that up in 1990 by confining diesel working to Saturdays only in July and August. That same year, *Alycidon* moved away, although it did return for brief stays in 1998, 2007, 2008 and 2013. By 1992, the editor of 'Moors Line' (No. 95) was able to confidently write: '…Track to run on, rolling stock to ride in and stations to commence and finish journeys are essential, but first and foremost it is the steam locomotive that visitors come to see.'

Nevertheless, the running of diesels and the holding of dedicated 'diesel galas' continued (and still does at the time of writing), and for younger generations

British Rail Class 55 'Deltic' No. D9009 *Alycidon*, photographed on 6 May 2007 pulling alongside Platform 2 at Grosmont, with Platform 1, part of the national rail network used by trains between Whitby and Middlesbrough, on the right. The Deltic was one of twenty-two that worked the principal expresses along the East Coast main line between 1961 and 1981. It was named after the 1949 Ascot Gold Cup winning horse, and after withdrawal in January 1982 was purchased by the Deltic Preservation Society. (Author)

who have never witnessed diesels at work on the national network, they have become as historically interesting as the steam engines they replaced.

Creating facilities for the restoration, repair and maintenance of locomotives has also involved NYMR management in some difficult decision making over the years. The area immediately south of Grosmont Tunnel was initially the only space where locomotives could be serviced and since then a fully equipped Motive Power Depot (MPD) and other restoration workshops have been

The 1973 Grosmont shed with its recently completed brick façade. Standing next to 'Tunnel Cottages' is John Fowler & Co. of Leeds 0-4-0 diesel-mechanical shunter No. 21, built in 1955 and converted into a diesel hydraulic in 1966, one of the many small industrial locomotives that were brought to the railway by various individuals and groups of enthusiasts in the 1970s. This particular one had worked for British Steel, Hartlepool, before remaining on the NYMR for twenty-seven years. (Author's collection)

Another powerful former NER locomotive to have worked on the NYMR is 0-8-0 Class T3 No. 901, seen here at Grosmont on 27 April 1991. The engine was built to a Sir Vincent Raven design in 1919, and was reclassified Class Q7 in LNER ownership. It worked from various sheds, was taken into British Railway stock in 1948, and not withdrawn until December 1962. It was preserved as part of the National Collection and in 1979 the NELPG began a major overhaul at Grosmont. In the year this photograph was taken, it achieved a mileage of 2,898 miles on the NYMR. (Author's collection)

Running into Pickering station in July 2002 is former Southern Railway 'Schools' Class 4-4-0 No. 30926 *Repton,* built in 1934. After withdrawal in 1962 it went to the Steamtown railway museum, USA, in 1966, before repatriation in 1989 and restoration at Grosmont. When this locomotive came to the NYMR it prompted a review of the track and bridges on the line as the engine had a heavier axle load than engines used up until then. (Author's collection)

LNER 0-8-0 Class Q6 No. 63395 again, this time making steady progress on the 1 in 49 climb through Darnholm on the approach to Goathland station, Sunday 15 May 2016. Behind the engine are six beautifully restored teak carriages, their colour complementing the lush spring greenery and the flowering gorse bushes. (Author)

Deviation signalbox, Grosmont, photographed on 12 October 1968. It had closed as a block post in 1930 but was retained as a ground frame under the control of ('released from') Grosmont signalbox and only used when access was needed to the Beck Hole branch line. (Tony Wickens/Online Transport Archive /2438)

developed there. The first steel-framed shed was erected between 1972 and 1973. Back then, the only buildings on the site were Deviation signalbox and a terrace of Victorian brick cottages that became volunteer accommodation. (The signalbox was the oldest on the line, dating from the forming of a junction between the original course of the Whitby & Pickering Railway and the new line through to Goathland Mill, opened in 1865.)

Despite this, as the need grew to provide more undercover accommodation for the storage, maintenance and overhaul of locomotives, the decision was made to demolish the signalbox in 1977 to make way for another locomotive shed ('Deviation Shed'). Four years earlier, in the Spring 1973 edition of 'Moors Line' (No. 23), the Civil Engineer had written in relation to the possible demolition: 'Do we preserve the box which is of no direct use to the railway or provide essential facilities for the historic steam engines on

the only site available?' Expressed here is the dilemma of railway preservation: preservation for its own sake, or preservation for use?

Deviation Shed, which came from the Longmoor Military Training Camp, was financed and built by the NELPG, the frame erected in May 1978 and the roof and cladding added during the summer. By 1982, there were twenty-nine locomotives on the Grosmont site in various states from working order to a kit of parts. The pressure to improve the facilities during that decade continued to be irresistible and by the start of the 1990s the site had been transformed into what looked something like a small MPD at the end of steam on British Railways.

In 1988, using Manpower Services Commission (MSC) labour, a new brick mess/amenity block was built on the north end of the 1973 shed. This block was officially opened on 29 October that year. By then the decision had been

Former NER 0-8-0 No. 63395 once again, this time resting alongside visiting ex-Somerset & Dorset 2-8-0 No. 53809 in Grosmont running shed on 3 April 2011. (Author)

made that the row of Victorian cottages that were still being used by volunteers had to go. In early 1989, the southern section was demolished, then at the end of July that year the last three occupants left, and between then and Christmas, the remainder of the row was cleared away so that the area could be used to store locomotive boilers. In October 1989, the only mechanical coaling tower on a heritage railway was brought into use close by, and in the New Year, a new running shed was constructed immediately to the east and adjoining the 1973 shed. In 1991, Deviation Shed was reclad and provided with better public access and was formally opened on 16 June of that year by NELPG President, Bill Harvey.

This rapid redevelopment of Grosmont MPD, lead to even more ambitious plans. In the summer 1989 edition of 'Moors Line' (No. 84) proposals were unveiled for the creation of a complex of workshops, museum displays and picnic areas on land to the south-east of the site that had been purchased in 1987. The complex was to be named the 'John Bellwood Museum' after the NYMR's one time General Manager and subsequent Chief Mechanical Engineer of the National Railway Museum, who had died in 1988. After the creation of the NYME plc in 1990 it was proposed to use some of the moneys raised through the share issue to finance this project, and although a start was made in July 1991 when the site was levelled by the Territorial Army, 'The John Bellwood Centre' as it had been rechristened progressed no further.

In 1997 a new fabrication shop partly funded by a European grant was erected in front of the 1973 shed, and then a few years later a brick structure was erected on the west side of the running lines to house Armstrong Oilers, a 1907 firm taken over by the NYMR in 2005.

British Railways Class 9F 2-10-0 No. 92214 under the coaling tower outside Deviation Shed, Grosmont on 15 April 2012. Following an overhaul the previous year it was named *Cock o' the North*, but did not stay on the NYMR for long, being purchased by a Great Central Railway plc director in 2014 and quickly moved to Loughborough. (Author)

The coaling tower next to Deviation Shed was brought into use in October 1989 as part of a major redevelopment of the area immediately south of Grosmont tunnel that had been first used at the end of the 1960s to prepare steam locomotives for their daily work. (Author)

Carriages

The story of carriage repair and restoration on the NYMR has also had its ups and downs. In the 1970s there was pressure to paint all the operational passenger carriages in a 'corporate livery' unique to the NYMR. To the relief of many railway enthusiasts, this did not happen, and since then vehicles have appeared in the liveries most appropriate to their original railway owners and their age. One of the best results of this policy has been the creation of a set ('rake') of beautifully restored LNER teak carriages.

The carcases of a number of these distinctive LNER vehicles had been some of the earliest arrivals to the NYMR, but the real impetus towards their restoration to original condition came in 1979. In that year the last remaining examples still owned by British Rail were put up for sale by tender. When the Council of the NYMHRT could not be persuaded to put in a bid, a group

of members of the Trust got together to form the LNER Coaching Association (LNERCA), one of their number immediately purchasing the group's first vehicle. They based themselves at Pickering to begin the laborious task of restoration. The group aimed for the highest standards of restoration, seeking out not just the correct replacement timber but also period fittings. Nothing upset them more than an innocent remark in the winter 1983/84 edition of 'Moors Line' (No. 66) that as there was an urgent need for more carriages LNER examples should be put back into revenue-earning service regardless of authentic fittings and livery!

At first the LNERCA was able to source a log of teak that was sawn to the lengths required for replacement panelling of a limited size. Then sheets of teak were imported from Bangkok and Singapore, allowing a number of LNER carriages to be restored not only at Pickering but also by other preservation

Behind Baldwin 2-8-0 No. 6046, five former LNER teak carriages all carefully restored at Pickering, form a train reminiscent of travel during the Second World War. The range from white to dark grey of the carriage roofs gives an indication of how long each vehicle had been in service. (Author)

societies at other railway heritage sites around the country. But the most interesting source of good timber was purchased in the late 1990s. This was a teak log, 40ft (12.2m) long with a cross-section tapering from 3ft (1m) to 2ft (0.6m) that had been recovered along with over 20 others from the wreck of the steamship *Pegu*, sunk on 8 July 1917 when it hit a British-laid mine during its voyage from Rangoon to Liverpool and Glasgow. Most of the logs were acquired for work on HMS *Victory*, but given that there was no chance of finding a similar log that could be cut into both the lengths and widths required to replace complete panels on LNER carriages, the LNERCA felt the asking price of £25,000 was a wise investment. The association's first LNER carriage was put back into traffic, fully restored, in 1994 (Gresley buffet No. 641) and ten years later members were looking after twenty-four wooden carriages dating from the 1890s to 1950, including seven LNER carriages running on the NYMR.

The restoration of other carriages by the NYMR's own small Carriage & Wagon team has not required the sourcing of material from such unusual locations, but it has involved them in an equivalent amount of painstaking work. For both groups, the task was eased in the 1980s by the erection of a 100ft (30m) long by 40ft (12m) wide two road shed and, ironically, the reinstatement of a

NYMR Trout Farm Carriage Stable at Pickering, completed in 2021 as part of the railways £10m Yorkshire Magnificent Journey Appeal funded by grants from the European Union, the National Lottery Heritage Fund, the Department of Environment Farming and Rural Affairs, the Local Enterprise Partnership and other donations. The structure provides undercover protection for up to 40 historic carriages. (NYMR/Charlotte Graham)

With locomotive and carriages all in authentic historic liveries, this 2013 view at Moorgates, just south of Goathland station, replicates perfectly a scene from the mid-1950s. Locomotive and carriages are a testament to the hard work of many volunteers over many years. (Author)

turntable at Pickering. Work started on the new building in the summer of 1983, and between then and 1996, a complex of buildings was created, funded from a number of sources, including Yorkshire & Humberside Museums & Art Gallery Service. The turntable project involved the excavation and enlargement of the existing pit and then the installation of the 60ft (18.3m) table from the National Railway Museum, rendered redundant in 1991 when 'The Great Hall' at York was being refurbished. (Many years before, the NYMR had salvaged a 55ft (16.8m) turntable from Neville Hill, Leeds, but had not been able to re-use it.) The work at Pickering was completed for the 1993 season.

No heritage railway can consistently run trains that replicate a specific historic period, but occasionally the date and liveries of the locomotive and the carriage behind do match, and this was just such a time at Grosmont on 11 May 2012. Visiting A4 No. 4464 *Bittern* in its 1937 livery was coupled to a train of five former LNER carriages restored to their original teak condition. (Author)

The most recent shed – The Atkins Building – was completed in 2008 and opened at the end of September that year by Pete Waterman. The public can access this building from the carpark and not only see progress on carriage restoration but also talk to the volunteers. Turning out and maintaining carriages in the most efficient way remains vital to the success of the NYMR, especially as all visitors travelling on the line will spend much of their time in these vehicles, which will leave them with a lasting impression of the railway.

Perhaps the ultimate travelling experience in NYMR carriages has been the Pullman services. By the 1980s authentic Pullman cars and modified and reliveried British Railways Mark One carriages had been brought together to form a 'Pullman' train. Although the fundamental concept of the premium service this train was able to provide has remained the same, the way it has been marketed and delivered has changed over the years. In the early 1980s the 'North Yorkshire Pullman' became very popular as an evening dining experience every Wednesday between May and September, running out and back between Pickering and Goathland. For the 1985 season the catering was contracted out and more carriages were added to the train so that more customers could be accommodated. A Thursday evening departure was added to the timetable and all services were extended so as to run the entire length of the line from Pickering to Grosmont. After further refurbishment of vehicles, other services were offered including a Sunday lunchtime train, 'The Moorlander', a Friday evening 'The Pickering Pullman', and a festive 'The Christmas Moorlander'.

At the time of writing, daytime services are marketed as the 'Kingthorpe Pullman', 'Moorlander Sunday Lunch' or 'Pullman Afternoon Tea', with evening

During the 2013 'LNER Gala Weekend', visiting twenty-first century A1 4-6-2 *Tornado* confidently climbs the 1 in 49 gradient at Water Ark on 6 October with the Pullman Dining Train. (Author)

The 10.30am departure from Grosmont behind A4 *Sir Nigel Gresley,* 5 October 2013. (Author)

trains advertised as the 'Pickering Pullman', 'North Yorkshire Pullman' and the 'Battersby Pullman Dining'. There are also special seasonal services and other occasional specials utilising the Pullman train, but what ever the manifestation and nomenclature, and in whatever form, it remains popular and is an important source of income for the NYME plc.

Stations

The standard of all NYMR stations also affects the visitor experience and here there is always tension between preservation and the provision of facilities demanded by twenty-first century families. During the 1980s the NYMR struggled with the basics such as toilets, ticket sales, shops and refreshments. The several, small, plywood kiosks erected on the platform at Pickering in the late 1970s to cope with some of these requirements were not popular but their use was defended in

the Autumn 1981 'Moors Line' (No. 57) article as 'regrettable but necessary'. Five years later they were removed along with the two BR Mark I coaches that had been parked at the south end of Platform 1 to provide refreshments.

As recorded elsewhere, passenger numbers continued to increase throughout the 1980s, not only putting pressure on station facilities but also in the way trains could be handled at platforms. The short, branch line platforms inherited by the NYMR could not cope with the length of trains and the volume of people using them. Extending the platforms was the sensible operational solution, but it had to be balanced against the dilution of the historic atmosphere of the stations. The public were drawn to the NYMR to savour that atmosphere and not just to get on and off trains as quickly and safely as possible. In 1988, plans for a major upgrade of the visitor facilities at Goathland station included suggestions to

An unusually quiet Goathland station photographed at the beginning of a new operating season in April 2013. The footbridge made up of standard cast-iron parts, is a good example of what became a familiar feature at many NER stations. This one, however, was not installed at Goathland until 1985, but it looks as though it has always been there. (Author)

During the Scottish Branch Line Gala weekend in May 2016, 'Black Five' 4-6-0 No. 45428 was given the number of another member of the same class – No. 45066 – and the shed plate 66A, to commemorate that locomotive's last years at Polmadie MPD, Glasgow. It was photographed on 14 May 2016 from a very popular photographic spot just south of Goathland station, pulling away with the 4.24pm to Pickering. (Author)

extend the down platform, which would have required the original NER signalbox to be rebuilt elsewhere. Fortunately, this was considered too great an alteration, and one no doubt management was pleased they had not backed when the visual appeal of the existing station was one of the deciding factors in ITV choosing to film many 'Heartbeat' scenes at the station.

Nevertheless, platform extensions were considered necessary at Grosmont and Pickering no matter the historic and visual impact. In 1989, BR completed the re-alignment of the Esk Valley line at the former so that the NYMR could extend Platform 2 northwards to accommodate ten-coach trains. The work was completed in stages, benefitting from the recovery of 115 stone platform coping stones from the redundant Helmsley station in March 1990 so that the job could be completed for the end of the year. Between May and August the following year, Platform 1 at Pickering was extended by contractors, and during 2003 Platforms 3 and 4 at Grosmont were extended.

As well as these changes, at Goathland and Pickering the NYMR also erected footbridges between platforms to reduce the use of the barrow crossings at these places that had always been a potential danger for both passengers and staff crossing the lines. Both these bridges were authentic NER cast-iron examples, the one

At the north end of Grosmont station a Northern Railways' train comes in from Whitby whilst on the right, the NYMR's train waits at Platform 2 for its timetabled slot with the 11.10am departure for the seaside town, 3 April 2016. The Esk Valley line here was realigned to allow the NYMR's down platform to be extended in 1990. (Author)

re-erected at Goathland in 1985/6 with financial assistance from Scarborough District Council coming from Howden station. The same pattern of footbridge for Pickering was acquired from Walker Gate, Tyneside, and was originally part of a plan to link the catering coaches parked next to an extended up platform to the down platform so that the barrow crossing could be eliminated at the south end of the station. Just over £2,500 was raised for this work, but the catering plan, along with the southern extension of the platform, was abandoned and, with the bridge project put on hold, the money went towards the Goathland bridge. The barrow crossing was eventually replaced by a new path around the buffer stops but a bridge between platforms north of the main station building was still useful as it would shorten the distance visitors had to walk from the car park (opened in 1981) at the west of the carriage works to the booking office on platform one. The bridge was brought into use in April 1997.

A number of authentic NER timber buildings have also been rebuilt at NYMR stations, successfully enhancing their environment. For example, at Pickering buildings from Gilling and Whitby have been re-erected, at Goathland a workshop was created from a warehouse from Whitedale station and at Grosmont, the booking office on Platform 2 came from Sleights. What completely transformed the whole environment of Pickering station for the better, however, was the installation of an overall roof to replicate the Y&NMR one that had been removed by British Railways in 1952. The work was part

of a larger project to refurbish all the surviving structures there. An appeal was launched in 1995 and a Heritage Lottery Fund (HLF) award of £330,000 was secured in 1998. With matching funds, this enabled the main stone buildings to be re-roofed, internal floors brought up to platform level, the booking office improved and other cosmetic upgrades achieved for the 2000 season. The final phase, which included the creation of a new learning centre and the fabrication and fitting of the overall roof, became possible following the award of an HLF grant of almost £1m, combined with support from the Regional Development Agency for Yorkshire and the Humber

The brand new overall roof at Pickering, receiving the final finishing touches in April 2011. (Author)

The authentic detailing of the braced trusses supporting the 2011 timber and slate roof at Pickering is a credit to the designers, as they had obviously taken much care in replicating those used for G.T. Andrews' original roofs at various stations on the Y&NMR. Unfortunately, since this photograph was taken, soot deposited from steam locomotives has obscured the subtle colouring of the individual components. (Author)

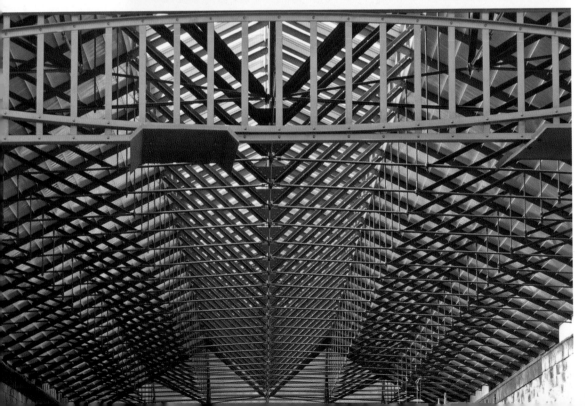

in September 2008. Sufficient matching public donations were forthcoming for work to take place through the winter of 2010/11, and fittingly, considering the outstanding quality of design and workmanship, the whole project gained the top award in the 2012 National Railway Heritage Awards sponsored by Ian Allan Publishing.

Civil Engineering and Permanent Way

In these areas of the NYMR's responsibilities, it is perhaps only signalling that is ever noticed by visitors. The majority will never see the bridges their train crosses during their journeys or the track on which it runs. But the maintenance and periodic renewal of these components of the railway is vital to the running of a safe service and it is in these areas that the biggest 'preservation' compromises have had to be made.

In 1973, the NYMR took over a line that was run down. There were thirty-seven bridges (including viaducts) and two tunnels, the masonry overbridges needing little attention but all the bridges made up either entirely of wrought-iron or of iron and timber in need of repair work. The single track (permanent way) that was inherited was mostly formed of 45ft (13.7m) and some 60ft (18.3m) lengths of bull head rail, supported in cast chairs, bolted to timber sleepers set in ash or very light ballast. On the tightest curves – and there were many – there was an additional line of rails called a 'check rail', positioned to help prevent wheel flanges of locomotives and rolling stock from riding up over the rail tops. At all the stations the layouts had been compromised by

Externally the new 2010–11 roof at Pickering was not an exact replica of the original 1845 one. The profile of the eaves was to the more generous proportions adopted by G.T. Andrews at Filey station where the roof had been restored in 2009. Photograph taken in April 2016. (Author)

British Railways 2-6-0 Class 4MT No. 76079 storming into Goathland station with a train from Whitby on 2 April 2016. It is running over traditional track made up of bullhead rail supported in cast chairs bolted to timber sleepers, the turnout in the foreground being laid by volunteers in the first years of the heritage line's history. The lower quadrant NER signal was also an NYMR addition, as was the earth bank at the end of the truncated former down line provided to stop any vehicle rolling down the 1 in 49 grade. (Author)

the removal of the second running line, and at Pickering, British Rail had made rushed rationalisations in between the cessation of passenger services and the end of coal traffic between there and Rillington Junction.

The tasks before the NYMR's new Civil Engineering Department were daunting, but the work was approached in a professional manner despite the limitations of volunteer labour. The priority was to make the NYMR infrastructure fit for purpose; preservation was a secondary consideration. Where

old equipment could not be repaired, it would be replaced with new because that was the way things were done on a professional railway.

During the winter of 1973, work started on altering the track layout at New Bridge, Pickering, and on installing a turnout at the north end of Levisham station to create a loop. The work was hard, relying on muscle power and camaraderie. Two years later, the crossovers at the summit of the line just south of Goathland, which had been used by engines running round their trains in the very early years of the NYMR, were removed. In the same year the first repairs were made to what was thought at the time to be steel decking plates in bridge No. 30 (see later). By 1977 the new track layout at Pickering was complete and had involved a lot of rearrangement, including the slewing of the track over High Mill crossing (up side to down side) and the taking out of the former down line at New Bridge level crossing and then slewing the track north of there to rejoin the remaining down track. In 1978, bridge No.10 near Farworth was the first to be fitted with a new concrete deck to replace the corroded metal one. Bridges 14 and 15 were similarly treated later in the 1980s. During February and March 1982, the track, ballast and infill of the arches of Esk Valley Viaduct (bridge No. 37) south of Grosmont, was removed so that a new waterproof membrane could be installed. In another major civil engineering exercise carried out between November 1987 and January 1988, bridges number 16 and 17, about three miles north of Levisham at Gallock Hill, were eliminated altogether by diverting Pickering Beck into a new channel. These are just a few examples of the achievements in just two decades of the NYMR's history, but the jobs were – and always will be – never ending.

By the end of the 1980s, the Civil Engineering Department had managed to develop a dedicated depot in a field owned by the NYMR at New Bridge for the equipment it had acquired since the 1970s (including track vehicles and a steam crane) and for the deliveries of rail, sleepers, etc. Work had started on this in the summer of 1982 when two sidings were run in off the main line. In 1987, planning permission was sought for a two road shed, which was initially refused by the North York Moors National Park Planning Committee. When the application was passed the following year, fund-raising began, but it was not until 1993 that work started on laying the foundations and erecting the frame of the shed. In the next few years, however, the site was extended and became to the Civil Engineering

Department what Grosmont MPD had become for the locomotive engineers, assuming all the qualities of a British Rail or Network Rail depot.

If proof was needed that civil engineering did indeed underpin the railway's operation, it came in the winter of 2009/10 when bridge No. 30 at Water Ark was replaced. The 1865 bridge over the Eller Beck at this remote location comprised a double-track, riveted, wrought-iron deck supported on stone piers either side of the river, which was crossed on the skew. It was the largest single metal span bridge inherited by the NYMR, and had been strengthened on a number of occasions and been carefully monitored since the 1970s. With the aim of maintaining the whole route for an axle load of twenty-two tons so as to allow the use of the largest main line steam locomotives, the ability of bridge No. 30 to cope with those loads had to be tackled. The decision was made to replace it with an uncompromising modern single track structure made up of steel beams supporting a concrete deck. The priority was to maintain the operation of the railway in the most efficient and practical way possible.

A £1m appeal was launched to raise the necessary money (which would also go towards the restoration of BR 2-6-4T Class 4MT No. 80135), attracting much high-profile endorsement and media coverage. As with all track renewals, the work had to be carried out during the closed season when revenue-earning trains were not running, and by 2009, that had narrowed down to a January. Contractors were employed to both dismantle the old bridge and erect the replacement, and their task was made almost impossibly difficult by heavy snowfall and freezing conditions. Despite this, removal was completed by the end of January and the new bridge was ready for the first passenger train of the 2010 season, which crossed southbound

Former LMS 'Black Five' No. 45428 crossing bridge No. 30 at Water Ark on 2 April 2016. The single track steel span bridge with cast concrete deck replaced the 1860s wrought-iron double track structure in the winter of 2010. As described in the main text, it was a challenging operation, not apparent from this view dominated by a hard-working locomotive. (Author)

on 27 March. As one of the prominent supporters of the project, Pete Waterman carried out the official opening ceremony on 19 April 2010.

The track relaid across bridge No. 30 was flat-bottom rail on concrete sleepers, a pattern and specification that had become the standard on the NYMR and on the national rail network. Concrete sleepers had become the preferred

replacement to traditional timber ones right at the start of the NYMR's involvement with the line.

Back in 1979 the Civil Engineer had reported in the Autumn edition of 'Moors Line' (No. 49) that his aim was to replace 4,000 timber sleepers each year for five or six years with concrete replacements. In reporting that flat bottom rail would be installed at Fen Bog, he went on to say: 'Flat bottom rail will last longer than bull head rail and hence in future, when we need to change the rail at the same time as the sleepers, we will endeavour to use this type of rail.'

By the end of the first decade of the twenty-first century, there was very little traditional bull head rail left in use on the running lines. Most of the check rails had been removed and ash had been superseded everywhere by stone ballast. There was much satisfaction felt by the civil engineering and permanent way teams in this achievement as there was in the next two logical advances made over the winter of 2014/15. At Beck Hole, as well as relaying with flat bottom rail on concrete sleepers, a three quarter mile long stretch was laid on steel sleepers with the rail welded up to form

A restored rake of former British Railways Mark 1 carriages, in matching late 1950s maroon livery, being hauled up the gradient at Water Ark by ex-LNER Class B1 on 6 October 2013. The train has just passed over a section of bullhead track on concrete sleepers that replaced the track inherited by the NYMR at this location, and is running onto a recently laid section of flat-bottom track carried on concrete sleepers. As elsewhere on the line, during relaying, stone ballast replaced the ash that once supported the sleepers. The track alignment was also altered slightly to take advantage of the double track formation. (Author)

continuous runs over that section. This latest innovation has not been without its critics, but the logic is undeniable: flat-bottom rail and matching track components can be acquired new, and eliminating rail joints every 60ft (18.3m) as with standard track, requires less maintenance, an important consideration

Visiting the NYMR in 2009, new-build 4-6-2 Class A1 No. 60163 approaches Levisham. Unlike at New Bridge, Pickering, the signalbox here survived with its lever frame intact and was subsequently re-locked to control the changed track layout developed by the NYMR's emerging S&T (Signal & Telegraph) Department in the 1970s. (Author)

on any heritage railway with limited human resources and particularly on one eighteen miles in length. How long traditional bullhead rail supported in cast chairs can or should be retained at NYMR stations is open to question.

Signalling

Although the signalboxes at Goathland Summit and those either end of Pickering station at High Mill and Bridge Street remained when British Railways closed the line, they did not survive into preservation. What did pass into NYMR ownership were the signalboxes at Grosmont, Deviation Junction, Goathland, Newton Dale, Levisham, and New Bridge (just north of Pickering). The fate of Deviation signalbox has already been chronicled.

The first signalbox to be brought back into use was that at Levisham, recommissioned on 10 May 1975 when the passing loop there had been completed. A number of original NER lower quadrant signals that had been brought in from elsewhere were made operational between then and the end of the summer season. With the opening of Levisham box, 'One Engine in Steam' working was introduced between there and Pickering. The following year, controversy was caused when lifting barriers with accompanying flashing warning road signals were brought

into use to protect the road crossing adjacent to the signalbox. These had been recommended after a Railway Inspectorate visit in 1972, and the work was financed by the County and District Councils as it was for their benefit and not an absolute requirement of the railway to provide this extra protection for what was officially only an occupation crossing.

Equally controversial was the provision of colour-light signals at Pickering a few years later. This decision had been made for purely operational reasons. The signalbox at High Mill crossing just north of Pickering had been demolished in 1970 but New Bridge signalbox a little further north had been listed as of historical importance by The Historic Buildings & Monuments Commission of England (English Heritage

As part of the Scottish Branch Line Gala for Sunday 15 May 2016, 'Black Five' No. 45428 was temporarily numbered No. 45049 and fitted with the shed plate 63B for Stirling, where that particular engine had been shedded between September 1956 and August 1963. It is seen here passing New Bridge signalbox at 9.45am with a demonstration mixed freight bound for Pickering yard. (Author)

after 1983) in November 1975. It was logical to re-use New Bridge for signalling purposes. British Rail had removed its eleven-lever, McKenzie & Holland frame and the wheel operating the gates before it closed the line, so the NYMR was able to make up a larger frame of twenty-one levers from McKenzie & Holland pattern parts and install this as well as a refurbished gate wheel. The re-signalling was planned as the new track layout was developed but it took some years to complete, between 1976 and full commissioning over the winter of 1985/86. As part of the work, High Mill became

The interior of New Bridge signalbox, Pickering, photographed in 2014. British Rail had removed the lever frame and all other instrumentation in 1965. The NYMR was not able to run trains into Pickering station until 1975, by which time all signalboxes there had been demolished. So the decision was taken to refit a lever frame into New Bridge to work new colour-light signals and electrically operated points between there and the station. The frame was made up of standard McKenzie & Holland components including a refurbished Samuel Dutton designed wheel to work the crossing gates. (Author)

The signalman at Goathland waits to collect the Grosmont Crossing–Goathland single line token from the fireman of 0-8-0 Class Q6 No. 63395 as it pulls into the station with the 5.15pm from Grosmont on 14 May 2016. The high visibility vest gives the twenty-first century footplate crew something to aim at. (Author)

an open crossing with flashing warning lights removing the need until then to employ a crossing keeper when trains were running.

By the 1980s, the NYMR had 'One Engine in Steam' in operation between New Bridge and Pickering station, 'Staff & Ticket' working between New Bridge and Levisham and between there and Goathland, with single line token working between Goathland and Grosmont Crossing using Tyers No. 6 tablet machines. The signalbox at the latter was a small hut next to Front Street level crossing, but it had been the intention to recommission the elevated signalbox at the north end of the station. To that end the signalbox interior had been cleaned in 1975 but then altered priorities halted any further work. With the focus then turned to a future extension of the platform, which would require British Rail to realign its track through the area

where the signalbox stood, the aim then became to resite it either adjacent to the road level crossing as an operational box, or on the platform as a museum piece. On 25 March 1979, the timber top (the operating room) was removed to the car park, and the remaining timber and brick base cleared away the following week. But again, priorities changed, funding was not available, and the plans were shelved. The operating room sat in the car park until October 1989 when it was dismantled and removed to Alston for possible reuse there.

Eventually, a completely new signalbox was erected immediately northeast of the level crossing at Grosmont using bricks recovered from Whitby Town's signalbox. The new structure was based on a NER Type SIa signalbox and was equipped with a fifty-two lever McKenzie & Holland frame and two gate wheels to work a reconfigured set

The NYMR-built signalbox adjacent to Front Street level crossing, based on a NER Type SIa (as classified by the Signalling Record Society in the 1970s), was commissioned for the May Bank Holiday in 1996, and photographed just a month short of the twentieth anniversary of that event in April 2016. (Author)

British Railways 4-6-0 Class 4MT No. 75029 entering Grosmont station from the south on 3 May 2014. The fabricated steel bracket supporting the upper quadrant semaphore signals on the right came from Whitby and was erected in its new position in the summer of 1989. Its partner on the left was salvaged from Consett and erected a little later that year. (Author)

Part of the metal lattice gantry from Falsgrave, Scarborough, supporting the semaphores controlling the north end of Grosmont station, photographed in April 2015. The signalling here was brought into use in July the previous year, improving access to and from the national rail network for NYMR trains working to and from Whitby. (Author)

The NER signals on the southern approach to Goathland station. The bracket was recovered from Glaisdale in January 1975 and craned into its new position on 2 October 1976. It was adapted to support the three signals needed to control the modified layout at Goathland necessitated by only a single track being retained between there and Levisham. The horizontal beams supporting the two shunting signals were replaced with new timber during the summer of 1990. The cast numbers screwed to the base of the post indicate which levers in the signalbox operate the three signals. (Author)

of crossing gates. It was brought into use along with a number of upper quadrant signals in May 1996 and won the Westinghouse Signalling Award in 2001. This impressive installation compensated in some way for the loss of the original Grosmont signalbox and the demolition in November 1994 of the remains of the signalbox at Newton Dale, which had long since been stripped of its lever frame and other equipment by British Rail. On a number of occasions it had been suggested that a passing loop should be laid at Newton Dale to break up the long single track section between Levisham and Goathland, but as the gradients where the box was located were not favourable, the loop would have had to be located elsewhere. The challenges of maintenance and security and the realities of manning such a remote signalbox with no operational purpose, sealed its fate.

On a more positive 'preservation' note, from the early 1970s, the NYMR had been actively collecting NER lower quadrant signals when British Rail were replacing them, and a number were salvaged and re-erected on the line. In 1974 the 25ft (7.6m) tall timber post with all its fittings was removed from Belmont Crossing, Harrogate. The following year, the post and cast-iron brackets from a signal at Glaisdale were salvaged and re-erected in a modified form to the south of Goathland station.

A further NER signal post and fittings were recovered by the York Group of the NYMR on 12 July 1977 from Wilstrop near Hammerton, where it was being replaced by a new distant signal. By the end of the 1970s, Levisham had seven operational authentic NER lower quadrant signals helping to balance out the comments of those who criticised the NYMR for installing modern colour-light signals at Pickering.

It is also interesting to compare the approach to the repair and replacement of these NER signals to that of permanent way. When the original posts and arms have had to be replaced because they were beyond repair, the purely practical, operational solution would have been to install upper quadrant semaphores on tubular metal posts, because they need less maintenance and spares are still readily available. The ultimate operational solution would have been to replace with colour-light signals! However, timber of the same proportions as the originals has been used and carefully formed to create replica NER signals. Obviously, this comparison has its limitations, but this author believes it is worth making.

Filming and Special Events

Many heritage railways have benefitted from being chosen by TV and film companies as shooting locations and the same has been true of the NYMR. For example, in 1992, £100,000 was earned from filming and passenger numbers were also given a considerable boost by the screening of what became one of television's classic series – 'Heartbeat'. Many locations in Goathland village, including the railway station, were used to create the fictional community of Aidensfield. The first episode was broadcast in 1992 and despite the Vice Chairman of the NYMR's subdued comment in 'Moors Line' for the summer of that year (No. 96) that 'The opening sequence each week shows a brief view of an NYMR train passing Fen Bog, and as some of the scenes show the Goathland area it may perhaps stimulate tourist interest', the series proved an instant and huge success. Before long, thousands of fans were making their pilgrimage to Goathland, and crowding onto NYMR trains.

For one dramatic episode broadcast in September 1993 involving a train crash,

NYMR timetable covers for the last five years of the twentieth century when the success of ITV's 'Heartbeat' series was helping to boost the NYMR passenger numbers and income to the levels experienced in the boom years of the late 1980s. (Author's collection)

a couple of carriages were strategically positioned outside Grosmont Tunnel to simulate the results of a derailment. The staging took place in January that year and in the following month one of the carefully damaged carriages was wrecked completely at Newton Dale Halt in a controlled explosion for the benefit of Central Television's 'Cook Report'. The purpose was to demonstrate the devastation that could be caused if a terrorist bomb exploded in a train. A useful £14,250 was made by the NYMR in fees from the TV companies and for the scrapping of the carriage.

Television and film work can be lucrative for the railway but it is not a guaranteed source of income. Since the 1980s what has become of major financial importance to the railway has been its regular and special events. Every year the NYMR stages themed days or weekends in order to attract return visitors. For railway enthusiasts, gala weekends are treated almost like annual pilgrimages, and for many families, Santa Specials are key to ensuring children's Christmas expectations are fulfilled. The increasing popularity of Halloween now rivalling Bonfire Night, has been of great benefit, dubious costumes and make-up being far less dangerous to stage than fireworks. In recent years the growing attraction of Second World War themed events has also provided another excuse for dressing up.

Hauling the 10.27am from Grosmont on 15 May 2016, the locomotive fireman obliges with a dramatic display of smoke for the photographers lined up at Darnholm just **north** of Goathland station. The 2-6-4T No. 80072 had been specially decked out as No. 80007, another member of its class, as part of the Scottish Branch Line Gala weekend, that latter locomotive having spent all its working life in Scotland at Polmadie and St Margaret's sheds. (Author)

Two former LNER A4 4-6-2s that entered service in the same year – 1937. No.4464 *Bittern* sports its 1930s Garter Blue livery, whilst behind, No. 60007 *Sir Nigel Gresley* (originally numbered 4498) is in early British Railways blue. Photographed at Grosmont during the 'Spring Steam Gala', May 2012. (Author)

On loan from the heritage Churnet Valley Railway, Baldwin Locomotive Company 2-8-0 No. 6046, built in 1945, double-heading with ex-LNER 4-6-0 Class B1 No. 61264 masquerading as another member of the same class, No. 61002, *Impala* on 5 October 2013 during the NYMR's 'LNER Weekend'. The two locomotives were making an easy, but noisy, job of climbing from Grosmont towards Beck Hole. (Author)

Showing no outward display of effort on the same stretch of line and on the same day as the Baldwin 2-8-0 and B1, ex-LNER 4-6-2 Class A4 No. 60007 *Sir Nigel Gresley* is hauling the dining train at Green End. (Author)

Whitby & Pickering Railway Revival

The surprisingly neat conclusion to this particular heritage railway story is that since 2007, regular passenger trains have been operated between Pickering and Whitby, reviving that railway service first introduced in 1836. It appears a logical achievement, but it has been both hard fought and controversial for the NYMR.

For a number of years after the Beeching cuts there was a period of paralysis throughout the British Rail network. Its trains and those of the NYMR ran into adjacent platforms at Grosmont station, but only the former were able to make the journey onwards to Whitby. Throughout the 1970s, Whitby Town station remained largely unaltered, with only the goods yard turned over for non-railway use. In 1972 the station buildings were designated Grade II on the list of historic buildings worthy of preservation, but then in the 1980s there was savage rationalisation. The line between Grosmont and Sleights had been reduced to a single track in 1972, but in 1984 the line between Sleights and

The 2pm departure from Whitby to Pickering photographed on 28 August 2014 from the A171 (Helredale Road) bridge with the River Esk to the left. (Author)

Whitby was also singled with only the former Platform 1 at Whitby remaining in use, with a section of the former up line retained as a sidings. The two signalboxes there (Bog Hall and Whitby) were closed.

Since the NYMR was formed, many people associated with that organisation had discussed whether or not running heritage trains into Whitby would be feasible some day. The severe cut-backs by British Rail in 1984 prompted more heart searching, and some believed the time was right to make Whitby the northern terminus of the NYMR by reinstating double track from Grosmont so that one line could be used exclusively for NYMR's trains. Ideas were aired for not only separate NYMR platforms at Whitby, but also engine and carriage sheds, and the reopening of the signalbox. If proof were needed that it was possible, then enthusiasts pointed to the SVR that had just extended to Kidderminster and was establishing an impressive terminus there, and to the Great Central Railway that was set to extend to a new railhead just north of Leicester. In November 1986, with the backing of Scarborough District Council and Whitby Town Council, it was decided to carry out a feasibility study into a possible extension of the NYMR. The Chairman of the NYMHRT felt any extension would over-stretch the resources of the railway, financially, in staffing levels and in motive power and rolling stock. When the report was published at the end of 1988 he must have been relieved to read it would indeed be operationally uneconomical to run to Whitby, although the social and economic benefits for the seaside town were felt to outweigh the problems. The report concluded that laying an extra track would be prohibitively expensive as British Rail had realigned its single track in many places, slewing the line across the former double-track formation. Axle loadings on bridges

was also highlighted as an issue. It was estimated the project would cost £2m. Another option of running steam trains over British Rail's single line was also considered uneconomical as British Rail required every train to be manned by its own staff and the pathing of trains run by an independent organisation was felt to be problematic.

British Rail did not want to invest in Whitby; it wanted to make money from the sale of its redundant land there, and in 1988 plans were submitted to Scarborough Borough Council for the building of a new supermarket on the site of Platforms 2, 3 and 4, with a new car park replacing the signalbox and remains of the goods shed. In 1990 a formal agreement was signed between the North Eastern Co-operative Society and the British Railways Board and work on clearing the site began. The NYMR was able to salvage 260 tons of facing stone and concrete coping slabs and was also given the option by the Co-op to dismantle Whitby signalbox as well. This was achieved during May and June 1990, leaving only the remains of the goods shed to be demolished by the contractors. The footprint of the new supermarket allowed just enough space for the reinstatement of a narrow Platform 2 in the future. Construction was rapid and the supermarket opened on 9 July 1991. Four months later, the 1847 engine shed with its 1868 extension immediately south of the station was listed Grade II by English Heritage to give that structure some protection from demolition.

As this relentless reduction in the railway infrastructure at Whitby added to inconvenient procedures necessary for through running between the NYMR and British Rail at Grosmont, it seemed the likelihood of a regular Whitby–Pickering service had been lost. Then came the privatisation of British Rail in 1994 and optimism returned, because that reorganisation brought with it the principle of open access, allowing any company to run their own trains almost anywhere on the national rail network provided they met certain operating standards. But the right to operate was still dependant on the state of the track and signalling, responsibility for which had passed from British Rail, firstly into the hands of Rail Track, and then to Network Rail. In 2003 the latter organisation assessed the track as too poor for the running of steam trains into Whitby by any operator.

Much lobbying followed and two years elapsed before the track was renewed. When that was completed, Network Rail allowed a limited steam-hauled service to be operated for the NYMR between Whitby and Glaisdale (with connections to the NYMR at Grosmont). The next step was for the NYMR to be allowed to run that service using its own footplate crews, and in January 2007 it became the first heritage railway to be granted a licence by the Office of the Rail Regulator to operate on the national rail network. With Network Rail support, the signalling at Grosmont was modified, and on 3 April 2007, the first NYMR service from Pickering ran to Whitby as the prelude to a regular service starting that Easter.

The 12.45pm **departure** from Whitby to Pickering on 28 August 2014 with Larpool Viaduct in the background. The footpath from which the photograph was taken was occupied by the up line until rationalisation in 1984. (Author)

Accelerating rapidly away from Grosmont on Saturday 14 May 2016 with the 2.46pm for Glaisdale, 2-6-0 No. 76079 had temporarily been given the number of an engine of the same class that had been based in Scotland. Other locomotives had similarly been renumbered as part of the NYMR's Scottish Branch Line Gala that month. (Author)

The increased mileage with all the attendant staffing issues and maintenance of engines and rolling stock to conform to the higher standards required to run on the national rail network, put a considerable strain on NYMR resources. Opinion was divided as to whether or not the effort was worth it. The 2008 season proved a challenge. Nevertheless, the NYMR management persevered and was given very positive support from all the organisations and local authorities involved in running and promoting the service. That level of support was such that within a few years all parties agreed to reinstate Platform 2 at Whitby. As two trains would then be able to occupy the station at the same time, this would not

only improve operational flexibility if trains were running late but also enable more trains to be run by either the national operators (Northern Rail at the time) or the NYMR.

At the beginning of 2013, £1.1m was made available via the Government's Coastal Communities Fund, with a further £850,000 coming from Network Rail. Work started in February 2014 on both the platform and associated new trackwork, the former used by the first paying passengers on 12 August

B1 No. 61264 again with another change of identity as No. 61034 *Chiru* (an alternative name for the Tibetan gazelle), running around its train at Whitby on 28 August 2014. The new track and platform are very obvious, having been in use for NYMR trains for only sixteen days when this photograph was taken. If justification for the investment was needed, the train was packed. To the right is a small section of the Co-operative supermarket that was built over Platforms 3 and 4. (Author)

2014 before it was officially opened four days later. In parallel with this project was another to improve the signalling at the north end of Grosmont station. Fortuitously, the re-signalling of Scarborough station took place in 2010, and conveniently, the requirement for Network Rail to preserve the metal lattice signal gantry adjacent to Falsgrave signalbox because it was part of the latter's status of Grade II Listed, coincided with the NYMR's need for such a structure in its re-signalling at Grosmont. Network Rail could be relieved of its obligation to preserve by

donating the gantry to the NYMR for 'preservation' at Grosmont. It went first to Invensis, the signalling contractor, at its Retford works for restoration, before being delivered to the NYMR in September 2012. By the end of that month, the shortened gantry had been re-erected at Grosmont with attention then focused on the timber signal posts (dolls) and all the relocking and electrical work necessary at Grosmont Crossing signalbox. The first stage of the project was completed at the beginning of July 2014 ready for the new Whitby service, and in the following year it was awarded the Siemens Signalling Award in the 2015 National Railway Heritage Awards, a fitting conclusion to this chapter, if not the whole story of the NYMR so far.

British Railways 2-6-0 Class 4MT No. 76079 bringing the 11.50am from Whitby into Grosmont's Platform 2 on 3 April 2016. It is passing the 'parachute' water column rescued from Derwenthaugh Junction near Gateshead and re-erected during 1990. Notice also the salvaged stone blocks used in 2003 when this platform was extended. (Author)

A view of the seven signals on the modified Falsgrave gantry at the north end of Grosmont station, brought into use in July 2014. The two main semaphores at the top the posts (or 'dolls') of equal height control entry on to the Esk Valley line (seen on the extreme left) from the NYMR's Platforms 2 and 3. The main semaphore on the right, on the shorter doll, is fixed at danger, indicating no train can pass from the NYMR's Platform 4 onto the Esk Valley line. All the smaller subsidiary or shunting signals beneath the three main arms control access to the sidings visible in the background. (Author)

Bibliography

The following is not a definitive list of all the books that have been written about the North Yorkshire Moors Railway, but a list of those used as references in the compilation of this book:

'Railways around Whitby', Martin Bairstow, published by the author, 1989

'The Scenery of the Whitby and Pickering Railway', H. Belcher, 1836

'An Illustrated History of the North Yorkshire Moors Railway', Philip Benham, OPC/Ian Allan Publishing, 2008

'North Yorkshire Moors Railway Stock Book 1990', N. Carter, North York Moors Historical Railway Trust, 1990

'Railways of the North York Moors', K. Hoole, Dalesman Books, 1983

'The North Yorkshire Moors Railway: a Past and Present Companion', John Hunt, Past & Present/The Nostalgia Collection, 2001

'Whitby and Pickering Railway', David Joy, Dalesman Books, 1973

'North Yorkshire Moors Railway: A Pictorial Survey', David Joy, Dalesman Books, 1991

'Guideline to the North Yorkshire Moors Railway', David Joy, North Yorkshire Moors Railway, 1998

'The North Eastern Railway, its Rise and Development', W.W. Tomlinson, Reid & Co., 1914

'North Yorkshire Moors Railway: A Pictorial Survey', Peter Williams & David Joy, Dalesman Books, 1977

'Official Opening by HRH The Duchess of Kent, May 1st 1973', souvenir booklet, 1973

Index

References to illustrations in **bold**

STATIONS AND LINESIDE VIEWS
— IN AND AROUND —
LONDON

B.W.L. BROOKSBANK
AND PETER TUFFREY

FONTHILL

Fonthill Media Limited
Stroud House
Russell Street
Stroud GL5 3AN

Fonthill Media LLC
12 Sires Street
Charleston SC 29403

www.fonthillmedia.com
office@fonthillmedia.com

First published in the United Kingdom
and the United States of America 2017

British Library Cataloguing in Publication Data:
A catalogue record for this book is available from the British Library

ISBN 978-1-78155-552-1

Typeset in Sabon LT
Printed and bound by CPI Group (UK) Ltd, Croydon, CR0 4YY

Acknowledgements

As the source of all the photographs, and an auxiliary with respect to the text, B. W. L. Brooksbank is keen to draw the recognition of the reader to his abundant and lasting gratitude to Peter Tuffrey. He has taken such an interest in B. W. L. Brooksbank's photographs, after seeing his images uploaded on to the Geograph.org.uk website, that he has not only used some of them in his recent series of books on railway stations of Yorkshire, but subsequently has been keen to collaborate with him in producing this book about London's railways.

The authors would also like to thanks the following people for their help: Doug Brown, Marian Crawley, Peter Jary, Hugh Parkin, Tristram Tuffrey.

London Bridge Station

The frontage of London Bridge station would be rebuilt in the mid-1970s and is presently undergoing major works. This picture was taken on 3rd October 1960 from the top of the steps up from St Thomas' Street to London Bridge Street and shows the Central Section station to the right and the Eastern Section ahead.

Clapham Junction 34094

Bulleid 'Light' Pacific no. 34094 *Mortehoe* heads south on the ex-L&SWR main line from Waterloo on 10 September 1960. The locomotive, constructed in October 1949, would not be rebuilt and was withdrawn in August 1964.

Contents

Introduction

London has been a place of great importance for 2,000 years, being the hub of England's commercial, financial and political activities. Therefore, transportation to and from the capital city has always been a necessity for the population. The railways, as a method of achieving this, became increasingly vital after their introduction to the area in the 1830s and remain so at the present time. Equally significant was the passage of freight, on a number of different routes, to the many marshalling yards and goods depots spread across the capital, but, unfortunately, this role has diminished since the early 1960s.

This book, which uses the modern boundary of the M25 to 'define' London, attempts to capture the many diverse railway scenes on offer in the immediate post-war period up to mid-1960s. This era was not only an interesting period for Britain, as the country recovered from the devastation and hardships caused by the Second World War, but for the railways. The 'big four' companies were Nationalised in 1948 to form British Railways and the organisation subsequently tried to cater for the population and their changing needs. In addition, the company had to come to terms with the necessity of either replacing steam motive power, which had been neglected during the War, or modernising completely with diesel or electric stock.

Improvements were not confined to locomotives as a number of stations and routes bore the brunt of BRs' unsentimental actions. One such high-profile casualty was Euston, which was completely demolished to make way for a new station with a larger capacity. This saw the loss of the Doric Portico and Euston Hotel as well as the Great Hall. Scenes before, during and after this process are included here, while, in contrast, King's Cross station remained little altered during that period. Some of the termini would be modernised later in their life, such as Waterloo, London Bridge, Liverpool Street and particularly St Pancras, leaving them perhaps unfamiliar to the traveller of today.

Also featuring in this collection of over 240 black and white photographs, all taken by B. W. L. Brooksbank, are many of the London Midland & Scottish Railway's, London & North Eastern Railway's, Great Western Railway's and Southern Railway's locomotive classes (and those of their pre-Grouping counterparts), which were used for both passenger and freight trains. Some of these were designed principally to work London express services, while others were built mainly for suburban traffic of which the capital had a great amount. BRs' Standard Classes also feature frequently in the album, as their numbers permeated the ranks of the established locomotives from the mid-1950s.

Several express engines were singled out for comparison after Nationalisation and a number of locomotives are presented here at mainline stations not otherwise visited by them. For example, O. V. S. Bulleid's 'Merchant Navy' Class Pacific no. 35017 *Belgian Marine* has been photographed leaving King's Cross station with an LMS-type tender and a dynamometer car. Also, Sir Nigel Gresley's record-breaking A4 Class Pacific *Mallard*, numbered E22 at the time, arrives at Waterloo after a run from Exeter.

Passenger classes are not only seen at stations but at a number of other points, such as beside running lines and from bridges. Peppercorn A1 and Gresley A3 Class Pacifics have been captured with trains to Leeds and Newcastle respectively at Hadley Wood, while 'Patriot' Class 4-6-0 no. 45536 *Private W. Wood, V.C.* is pictured with an express from Manchester at Cricklewood and 'Merchant Navy' Class no. 35016 *Elders Fyffes* takes a relief express service through Wimbledon.

The suburban lines were as important to the capital's transport system as the main routes. In the mid-nineteenth century, after the central area had received tracks, routes spread out to the then sparsely populated suburbs. Often before or after a rail connection was made with the city, new houses would spring up in the once idyllic countryside, as speculators prayed on this convenience. A number of these lines were electrified during the early twentieth century, while others were not converted until as late as the 1980s. Balham station was transformed during a large-scale scheme begun before the start of the First World War, but Enfield Town station saw steam locomotives transporting commuter services until 1960.

Freight trains have not been neglected and form a good portion of the pictures included here. The traffic to the capital was quite varied, ranging from milk, seen at East Acton and Vauxhall, and coal, pictured behind Class 9F 2-10-0s at Harringay and New Southgate, to parcels at Southall and West Ealing. A scene has been captured at Feltham marshalling yard, which was built by the London & South Western Railway in the early 1920s to handle all of the company's goods traffic in and out of London, and locomotives are pictured at Harringay after leaving Ferme Park marshalling yard with trains formed there.

As London hosted a number of events, special trains would often be scheduled to cater for them. One such example is the FA Cup final and locomotives from Nottingham, Derby and Burnley have been recorded at Wembley station and Neasden after bringing supporters to the stadium. The railways of London could attract specials in their own right, as demonstrated by the inclusion of the Railway Correspondence and Travel Society's East London Tour of 14 April 1951. Holden J69 Class no. E8619 was employed as one of the engines for the excursion and is pictured at Fenchurch Street station.

Moving on to the possibly mundane, but necessary, task of transporting coaching stock to and from the carriage sidings; several locomotives are pictured when employed on this duty and many are at the main line termini, but a number are also seen at Clapham Junction carriage sidings on or between movements. Another essential function was the housing and maintenance of the engines that worked London's trains. More than a few of the depots around the capital were visited and the motive power there recorded. Being in the midst of a large goods station, Bricklayers Arms had several freight locomotives present during April 1959, while Neasden had two classes of suburban tank engines on view when trips were made to the shed in 1948 and 1957.

With such an interesting and varied mixture of stations and locomotives to be seen in and around London, the authors hope that their selection of photographs enthrals the reader as much as they have been while compiling this book.

Stations and Lineside Views
In and Around London

Balham Station

Balham station was opened as Balham Hill on 1 December 1856. The station was on the route between Wandsworth Common and Crystal Palace (Low Level), which was built by the West End of London & Crystal Palace Railway. The London Brighton & South Coast Railway worked, then took over the WE&CPR and moved the station during major redevelopments, completed in 1863. These entailed the diversion of the route from south of the Thames at Pimlico over Grosvenor Bridge to Victoria station. Meanwhile, a cut-off from Windmill Junction (Croydon) to Balham was opened in December 1862, becoming the main line to Clapham Junction and Victoria from Croydon and beyond. The Southern Railway changed the station's name to Balham & Upper Tooting on 9 March 1927 and by September 1929 the company had converted all the lines electrified by the LB&SCR, with their 6.6 kV overhead wires, to the 600v DC third-rail system. The station's name reverted to plain 'Balham' on 6 October 1969. This picture, taken on 2 March 1961 looking east towards Crystal Palace (left) and Croydon (right), shows the main railway station with an up train stopping at the platform.

Barking Station

Barking station is shown facing eastward on 12 May 1961. This was a short time after the station was comprehensibly rebuilt with fly-overs and a fly-under to allow a ready flow of freight, from Ripple Lane Yard—and elsewhere—down the Tilbury line to the west and north, over the main commuter lines. The platforms served (left to right): down Kentish Town arrival, down and up District (Upminster) Line, down and up Tilbury and Southend lines, and up Kentish Town line; an ex-WD 2-8-0 is standing at the latter. The Fenchurch Street to Tilbury, Southend and Shoeburyness lines were electrified just six months later.

Barking 2511

Looking westward from Queen's Road bridge on 25 September 1948 and a Fenchurch Street to Shoeburyness train approaches Barking station. Stanier 3-cylinder 2-6-4T locomotive no. 2511, which was part of the class designed for working the LT&SR lines, is at the head of a train featuring old coaching stock. The Tottenham & Forest Gate Railway lines to/from Kentish Town are on the far side, beyond the London Passenger Transport Board District/Metropolitan tracks. No. 2511 was withdrawn in July 1962.

Barkingside Station

This photograph was taken at the start of April 1961 on the south side of Barkingside station looking towards Newbury Park and London. From 31 May 1948 the stop was on London Transport's Central Line (Hainault Loop), but until 29 November 1947 Barkingside had been on the LNER (ex-GER) Fairlop Loop between Ilford and Woodford. The station has a typical Great Eastern appearance and has been little altered from that time, apart from the addition of 'Underground' signs.

Barnehurst Station

The Bexley Heath Railway opened Barnehurst station on 1 May 1895. The line formed two connections with the North Kent route; just east of Blackheath to the west and a triangular junction was present between Erith and Dartford near Slade Green. This scene was captured on 3 March 1961, with the camera pointing eastward.

Above: **Barons Court Station**

A train running on the Piccadilly Line stops on the westbound platform at Barons Court station with a service bound for Uxbridge. The station also accommodates District Line services and was opened by the District Railway on 9 October 1905..

Opposite page, from top to bottom:

Barnes Station

Barnes station was the product of the Richmond Railway, which, in the early 1840s, resolved to construct a line from a junction with the London & South Western Railway at Battersea to Richmond. Noted engineer Joseph Locke oversaw the project to completion in July 1846, with the public opening occurring on the 27th. The red brick 'Tudor gothic' station house, out of view past the road bridge on the right, is the only one of the line's five original stations to survive and is Grade II listed.

Battersea Park Station

The service from Beckenham Junction via Crystal Palace has stopped at Battersea Park station on the way to Victoria. The South London Line (to London Bridge via Denmark Hill) can be seen curving away on the left.

Barnes Bridge Station

The Windsor, Staines & South Western Railway was authorised to build an extension from the RR's route at Richmond to Windsor in 1847. As part of this act the company was also given powers to produce a line leaving the RR at Barnes, and running through Chiswick, Kew, Brentford and Hounslow, to join the new route at Feltham. This latter, becoming known as the Hounslow Loop, did not have Barnes Bridge station, pictured here on 7 May 1961, added until 12 March 1916 when the line was electrified

Bayswater Station

A bustling street scene in Queensway, Westminster, looking north from the corner of Inverness Place, serves as the backdrop for this picture of Bayswater station, taken on 11 March 1961. Opening had been carried out by the Metropolitan Railway on 1 October 1868 after the completion of the company's project to link Paddington Praed Street with Kensington.

Beckenham Hill Station

The Catford Loop between Brixton and Shortlands had five stations when opened in July 1892, one being Beckenham Hill, which has been photographed from Beckenham Hill Road bridge on 28 August 1962.

Beckenham Junction Station

On the right, in one of Beckenham Junction's two bay platforms, is a service bound for Victoria via Crystal Palace. The station was connected with the WEL&CPR extension line from Bromley Junction to Bromley (later Shortlands) upon opening on 3 May 1858. The station had commenced serving passengers only 18 months previously, as Beckenham, and was the terminus for the Mid Kent Railway line from Lewisham. 'Junction' was added on 1 April 1864 to avoid uncertainty with New Beckenham station, which was brought into use when the MKR extended the route to Addiscombe.

Berrylands Station

A down local train approaches Berrylands station on 15 February 1961. The station was a late addition to the line between Waterloo and Southampton in October 1933, being located between New Malden and Surbiton, after a large number of new homes were built in the area.

Above: **Beddington Lane Station**

View westward towards Mitcham Junction and Wimbledon on the Wimbledon to West Croydon line, taken at Beddington Lane station on 12 March 1961. The Wimbledon & Croydon Railway received an Act for the working of the line in 1853 and construction was carried out as a private enterprise, this being finished in October 1855. The route boasted just two new stations; Mitcham and Beddington, although the latter opened a short time later in early 1856. Beddington was some two miles from the village and the addition of the 'Lane' to the title was forced by locals in January 1887. Since 30 May 2000 the name has been in use for the stop on the Wimbledon Branch of the Croydon Tramlink as the original station closed on 1 June 1997 and was demolished.

Opposite page, below:

Bethnal Green Station 69602

A Liverpool Street station to Chingford local train climbs up the bank into Bethnal Green Station on 18 July 1959. At the head of the service is N7/4 no. 69602, one of original Great Eastern Railway Hill L77 Class 0-6-2Ts. The locomotive was modified in June 1949 to employ a round-top boiler and was the last of the GER class members to be so treated, the remainder acquiring the type during the 1940s. Nearly all of the 120 N7s were allocated to Stratford shed and were the mainstay of the intensive local services from Liverpool Street. The train is just turning on to the Cambridge main line via Hackney Downs. Note that white discs are being used as head code indicators. The picture dates from 18 July 1959 and no. 69602 would be withdrawn by the end of the month.

Above: **Bethnal Green Station 61203**
Having pounded up the 1,200 yards of 1-in-70 gradient from Liverpool Street station to Bethnal Green, the 11.24 to Hunstanton is about to turn sharp left on to the Cambridge main line for King's Lynn. There, the train would have to reverse to reach Hunstanton, where arrival was scheduled for 14.30. The locomotive is Thompson B1 Class 4-6-0 no. 61203, which was built in June 1947 and remained active until July 1962.

Above: Bickley Station

A Dover Marine to Victoria electric express train passes on the up main line while Bickley station is pictured at the beginning of March 1961. The station started life as Southborough Road on 5 July 1858 as the terminus for the South Eastern Railway's short line from New Bromley, later Shortlands.

Opposite page, from top to bottom:

Bethnal Green Station 61615

As part of major improvements to the lines between the new Liverpool Street station and North East London, the GER added Bethnal Green Junction station to the system on 24 May 1872. This was just prior to the opening of the new route to Stoke Newington, which left the main line just east of Bethnal Green. LNER Thompson B2 Class 4-6-0 no. 61615 *Culford Hall* heads at speed off the bank from Liverpool Street to the junction for the lines to the north on 30th August 1958. The train is the 12.14 Summer Saturday Liverpool Street to Hunstanton express which reached the Norfolk coast at 15.54.

Bexleyheath Station

The station preceding Barnehurst on the Lewisham to Dartford line was Bexleyheath. At the behest of one of the BHR directors, who was a prominent local landowner, the station was situated in a cutting—a quarter of a mile away from a more suitable location, where the goods yard was to be found. The main reason for this was that the surrounding land was envisaged for erection of new dwellings. However, this did not occur for some time as, the construction projects spread down the line from the west gradually until reaching Bexleyheath in the 1930s. The building boom was spurred on by the electrification of the BHR line by the Southern Railway in the mid-1920s; the installation of the footbridge seen in this picture, taken on 3 March 1961 looking east, dates from that period.

Bingham Road Station

The Woodside & South Croydon Railway completed a line between Woodside, on the Mid Kent line, and Selsdon Road station, on the Oxted route, during August 1885. Only one station existed initially, until two halts were added in the early twentieth century; one was Bingham Road. Due to poor usage, services were removed in 1915, but were reinstated after the SR electrified the line in 1935. £10,000 was spent building a station at Bingham Road, which remained in use until 16 May 1983. Subsequently, the route was utilised, at road level, by Croydon Tramlink.

Black Horse Road Station

View westward on 1 April 1961, towards South Tottenham, from Black Horse Road station on the ex-Tottenham & Forest Gate Railway line, which was a joint venture between the Midland Railway and London, Tilbury and Southend Railway. The name was changed to plain Blackhorse Road in May 1980, a little over a year before the station closed on 14 August 1981. A new facility was opened a short distance to the west for interchange with the Victoria Line.

Borough Station

Here is a scene captured during March 1961 looking southwest from the corner of Borough High Street and Great Dover Street to Borough station, at the junction of the former and Marshalsea Road. The station was opened by the City & South London Railway in December 1890 and was later absorbed into the Northern Line (via Bank).

Bow Station

Bow station's entrance, on the north side of Bow Road, is seen here on 12 May 1961. This was all that remained of the large hall and station built in 1870, which replaced the original East & West India Docks & Birmingham Junction Railway's building opened with the Islington to Bow line in 1850. The station fell victim to enemy action in May 1944 and never reopened, while the hall continued to thrive until the mid-1950s when consumed by fire. The entrance was then employed as a parcels office, but was closed in 1965 and then demolished.

Bow Road Station

The remains of Bow Road station, on the corner of Addington Road and Bow Road, are viewed from near the corner of Arnold Road on 12 May 1961. The station was opened by the GER on 1 October 1876 on the line from Fenchurch Street to Bow Junction (Stratford), but slightly to the south of the location here. Bow Road station was moved in 1892 to allow access to Bow station, just to the east (right). Closure of the former occurred between April 1941 and December 1946 as a result of bomb damage, and again, for building work, from January to October 1947, before passenger services were finally removed in November 1949.

Bow Road Underground Station

The Transport for London station is located only a short distance away from the ex-GER station to the west and on the south side of Bow Road. The station is pictured, when the aforementioned authority was branded the London Transport Board (1963–1970), at platform level, looking eastward, on 12 May 1961. District and Hammersmith & City Line trains serve Bow Road station, which has been Grade II listed since 1973.

Brentford Central Station

Brentford station was one of the stops on the Hounslow Loop line when opening occurred on 22 August 1850. A goods yard was provided at this time, as were similar facilities at Chiswick and Hounslow. The change in name was made on 5 June 1950 and remained in use until 12 May 1980, when the title reverted to Brentford after the closure of the ex-GWR station on the branch from Southall to Brentford Dock.

Bricklayers Arms Shed 31071

Shortly after his appointment in September 1898, the South Eastern & Chatham Railway's Locomotive and Carriage Superintendent Harry S. Wainwright began producing a design, with the help of Chief Draughtsman Robert Surtees, for a new 0-6-0 goods locomotive. A total of 109 C Class were produced between 1900 and 1908. No. 31071 was one of nine erected at Ashford Works in 1901, being completed in July. The locomotive was close to the end when pictured at Bricklayers Arms shed on 30 April 1959 as withdrawal happened in September.

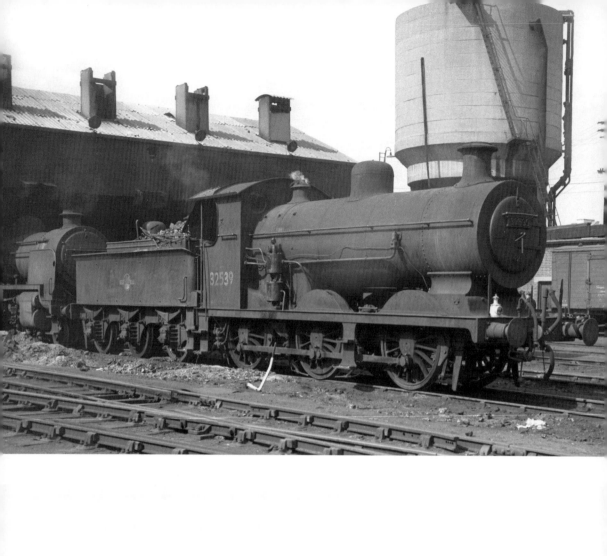

Above: **Bricklayers Arms Shed 32415**
R. Billinton E6 Class 0-6-2T no. 32415 has been photographed in the remnants of the 'new' shed, which was built in 1869 and damaged during the Second World War. The building was not repaired afterwards, later being used to store engines. Behind the locomotive is the repair shop which was built in the 1930s as part of large-scale improvements at the depot; a water softener (seen on page **xx**) and 65 ft turntable (just visible behind no. 32415) were also added at this time. The repair shop was one of the biggest at a depot in the London area and could undertake a variety of tasks.

Opposite page, from top to bottom:

Bricklayers Arms Shed 32539
The large locomotive depot at Bricklayers Arms, which was in the midst of the complex of goods stations and yards off the mile-long branch from the main lines at the North Kent Junctions in Bermondsey, still had a substantial complement of steam engines in April 1959, when these photographs were taken. LB&SCR R. J. Billinton C2X Class 0-6- 0 no. 32539 was one of seven class members allocated to the depot at this time.

Bricklayers Arms Shed 31851
Outside the four-road shed, which dated from 1865 and adjoined the original four-track structure opened in 1847 (seen here on the right) collectively known as the 'old' shed, is Maunsell N Class 2-6-0 no. 31851. The locomotive was built in February 1925, largely, at Woolwich Arsenal, but assembly occurred at Ashford Works. The former made a number of components for the class after the end of the First World War and sold parts for 50 locomotives to the SR after Grouping.

Above: **Bricklayers Arms Goods Station**

The South Eastern Railway and the London & Croydon Railway joined forces in the early 1840s to break the hold that the London & Greenwich Railway had on the line into London Bridge station. The two companies built a one mile-long branch line from the L&GR route at New Cross to a new terminus at Bricklayers Arms, Bermondsey. The station opened for traffic on 1 May 1844. However, the resultant loss of revenue forced the L&GR to agree to more favourable terms with the SER and L&CR and the companies stopped using the station from October 1846 and March 1845 respectively. The SER then developed the site as a goods depot and engine shed. The LB&SCR, as successor to the L&CR, later developed facilities on the site, which were named Willow Walk until 1932 when the goods station merged with Bricklayers Arms goods depot. This view south-eastward was taken inside one of the several loading-banks of the extensive goods depot on 30 April 1959. Closure came on 1 August 1977 and the site has been redeveloped.

Opposite page, from top to bottom:

Brixton Station

View south-eastward to Herne Hill at Brixton station. The London, Chatham & Dover Railway opened the facilities on 6 October 1862, but in the following year changed the name to Brixton & South Stockwell and this was applied until 9 July 1934. In 1864 the LC&DR opened the City Branch from Herne Hill to Blackfriars Bridge and a connection was made with Brixton station via Loughborough Junction, the tracks to which are seen on the left. The South London Line crosses over the girder bridge on the right, going towards Battersea Park and Victoria.

Above: **Bricklayers Arms Shed 32107**

L. B. Billinton Class E2 0-6-0T no. 32107 seems to be abandoned at Bricklayers Arms 'new' shed in April 1959, but the engine returned to work in October at Three Bridges. This was only a brief residency, however, as in February the following year a move to Southampton Docks occurred and no. 32107's career would come to an end there, becoming the first class member to be sent to the scrapyard in February 1961. Before arriving at Bricklayers Arms shed in May 1957, the locomotive had long been at Stewarts Lane depot, Battersea.

Above: Broad Street Station

The East & West India Docks & Birmingham Junction became the North London Railway in 1853. Just under ten years later in July 1861, the company's Act for an extension line from Dalston Junction, on the Islington–Bow line, to a new terminus station in Broad Street was given Royal Assent. NLR trains had previously been directed via the London & Blackwall Railway's line to Fenchurch Street station. The new, and impressive, NLR station was ready for traffic on 1 November 1865, with three approach lines and seven platforms. The venture was an immediate triumph with the public, swelling passenger numbers to well over 10 million a year in the period immediately after opening. A two-tier goods station was completed along the eastern side of Broad Street in May 1868. Improvements were implemented in the passenger part during the early 1870s with the addition of a fourth approach line, and again in the 1890s with the installation of another platform and the staircases to the concourse at the front of the building. Despite the initial success of Broad Street, a decline set in after the turn of the century. The station was hit during the Second World War, through bomb damage and the closure of the line to Poplar, and continued to see falling passenger numbers into the 1960s when threatened with closure by Dr Beeching. The inevitable was delayed until 30 June 1986 and the Broadgate office development has been built on the site.

Opposite page, below:

Bromley North Station

The terminus for the ex-South Eastern & Chatham branch from Grove Park, Bromley North is still an active London suburban station (electrification was carried out in 1926). Goods facilities, in evidence in this picture taken on 2 March 1961, have long since disappeared, after being removed on 20 May 1968.

Above: **Bromley Station**

View eastward, towards Barking, along the London Transport Executive electric lines at Bromley station on 12 May 1961. On the right are the tracks heading out to Tilbury and Southend. Bromley station had been opened by the London, Tilbury & Southend Railway on 31 March 1858 when the company opened a new line between Barking and Bow, which reduced the distance to Fenchurch Street station. The District Railway began operating services to Bromley upon the completion of the Whitechapel and Bow line in June 1902. On 27 October 1940 main line trains ceased to stop at the station and electrification, with overhead lines, occurred in 1962. However, Bromley was still under the guidance of British Railways at this time and transfer to the LTB did not happen until 1 January 1969. Meanwhile, in 1967, the station had been renamed Bromley-by-Bow.

Bromley South Station

Bromley South station, photographed from the east side looking towards London (Victoria and Holborn Viaduct stations) is an important suburban station on the Chatham and Kent Coast main line. Most trains run from Victoria as Holborn Viaduct services ceased in January 1990 and have since run from Blackfriars. 'South' was added to the name on 1 June 1899; Bromley North also received the addition at this time.

Brondesbury Station

The Hampstead Junction Railway was promoted to connect Willesden with the NLR at Camden in the early 1850s and the project came to fruition at the end of the decade. One of the stations on the line was Brondesbury, which was known as Edgeware Road Kilburn [*sic*], and several other variations, until the above was settled on in May 1883. In the distance, looking north-east, the overbridge carrying the six Metropolitan and LNER (ex-Great Central Railway) lines into Baker Street and Marylebone can be seen.

Bruce Grove Station
This scene was captured on 1 April 1961 from Tottenham High Road looking to Bruce Grove station, with the line coming over the bridge from Liverpool Street (left) and going towards Seven Sisters and Enfield Town. A trolleybus to Wood Green is seen in the distance; the route would be removed from 19 July 1961.

Buckhurst Hill Station
A Central Line train bound for Epping has stopped at the platform of Buckhurst Hill station, which was transferred from BR to LPTB on 21 November 1948.

Above: **Charing Cross Station 30926**

Maunsell V, or 'Schools', Class 4-4-0 no. 30926 *Repton* stands in readiness at the head of the 10.25 Hastings express, pictured at platform one, on 20 April 1957. The South Eastern Railway built the station and trains began to arrive from 11 January 1864, but not from the main line until 1 May. Charing Cross was closed between 5 December 1905 and 19 March 1906 after the original single span roof collapsed and the replacement of the entire structure was necessary. *Repton* was constructed at Eastleigh Works in May 1934 and was withdrawn in December 1962, but has since been preserved, being housed at the North Yorkshire Moors Railway where the locomotive is currently undergoing an overhaul.

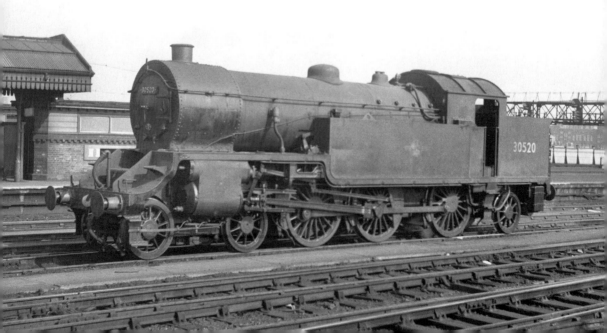

Above: Clapham Junction 42071

Strath Terrace provides the vantage point for this photograph of Fairburn 4MT 2-6-4T no. 42071 which is at the head of the 14.08 from Victoria to Tunbridge Wells West on 2 April 1958. The locomotive was constructed at Brighton in November 1950 and remained in service until March 1967. During this time the engine was Southern Region-allocated from being built until December 1959 with residencies at Stewarts Lane, Ashford, Ramsgate, Brighton and Three Bridges. Afterwards, no. 42071 went to the London Midland Region and worked from Bletchley, Willesden and Trafford Park.

Opposite page, below:

Clapham Junction Station 30520

Resting at the London end of the main line platforms at Clapham Junction station is London & South Western Railway Urie 'H16' Class 4-6-2T no. 30520. The locomotive is on duty moving empty coaching stock from the very large carriage depot located between the two sides of the station and Waterloo.

Above: **Clapham Junction 30903**
Another scene captured from Strath Terrace, looking eastward, towards Clapham Junction station. Maunsell 'Schools' Class 4-4-0 no. 30903 *Charterhouse* (built April 1930, withdrawn December 1962) is on the ex-L&SWR main line to the West; on the right is the ex-LB&SCR main line from Victoria to East Croydon and Brighton. The train was noted at the time as empty coaching stock, but the engine has the head code for the Salisbury line, so the service might be the 11.54 semi-fast from Waterloo running late.

Opposite page, from top to bottom:

Clapham Junction 32551
A freight train, off the West London Extension Line hauled by Billinton C2X Class 0-6-0 no. 32551, struggles on to the Brighton section in a cloud of steam at Clapham Junction station. The locomotive was erected at Vulcan Foundry in February 1902, but was rebuilt by D. E. Marsh in February 1909 with a larger boiler and smokebox, being one of the earliest transformations to C2X specifications. The engine is seen from platform 15/16 during early April 1958; partially in view on the left is Clapham Junction 'B' Box, controlling the Central (ex-LB&SCR) lines.

Clapham Junction 31616
SR Maunsell UClass 2-6-0 no. 31616 takes empty stock for a special service out of Clapham Junction carriage sidings on 4 July 1959. The locomotive (constructed September 1928, condemned June 1964) was allocated to Guildford shed at this time and had been there since April 1954, but would soon transfer to Redhill in January 1960.

Clapham Junction Station 4681

For a few years in the 1950s, several ex-GWR 0-6-0PTs were brought in by BR to help with the Clapham Junction–Waterloo empty stock workings. Collett 8750 Class engine no. 4681 was built at Swindon Works in November 1944 and arrived at Nine Elms in October 1959 from Danygraig. The locomotive was later at Feltham from April to October 1963, then returning to 'home' territory at Bristol Bath Road and was withdrawn there during December 1963. No. 4681 has passed under 'A' signal box which controlled all the trains to and from Waterloo.

Clapham Junction Carriage Yard 34024 and 30517

This picture has been taken from the down Windsor line platform, looking south- eastward across the carriage yard to the main station on 25 August 1962. Between empty stock workings to Waterloo are two light engines: rebuilt Bulleid 'Light Pacific' no. 34024 *Tamar Valley* and Urie H16 Class 4-6-2T no. 30517.

Clapham Junction 75077
View north from Battersea Rise, towards Clapham Junction, with the 13.54 Waterloo to Basingstoke semi-fast travelling past; BR Standard Class 4MT 4-6-0 no. 75077 (built in December 1955, surviving until July 1967) is in charge of the train. Climbing up on the right, and curving off to the east is the ex-LB&SCR main line from Victoria.

Clapham Junction Station 30517
Urie's H16 Class were introduced to work transfer freight services between Feltham and the other yards around London. However, in the 1950s a number of class members could be spotted working 'E.C.S.' trains from Clapham Junction. No. 30517 has been pictured undertaking such a duty on 25 August 1962 (and is also seen on p.36). 'B' signal box, which was responsible for Victoria Line trains, is on the right.

Clapham Junction Station 212

Ex-L&SWR Adams O2 Class no. 212, which is attached to a shunter's tool wagon at Clapham Junction on 26 April 1947, was one of the regular carriage pilots during this period. The O2s were designed for working London suburban trains, but were later displaced to branch lines as electrification took hold. No. 212 managed to hold a place in London until the late 1940s when transferred to Bournemouth.

Cricklewood Station 1207

Ivatt 2MT 2-6-2T no. 1207 is seen working a St Pancras to St Albans local service at Cricklewood station on 18 June 1948. The locomotive had only recently been added to LMS stock in December 1946 and is still wearing the company's livery. From January 1949 the engine would carry BR no. 41207 until withdrawal in November 1966.

Cricklewood 148 and 2681

A down empty stock train from St Pancras is photographed at Watling Street Junction, near Cricklewood; off to the right are West End Sidings. The train is headed by two tank engines: Stanier 3P 2-6-2T no. 148 (built 1937, withdrawn August 1962) and Fairburn 4MT 2-6-4T no. 2681 (built 1945, withdrawn March 1965).

Cricklewood Station 34

Fowler '3P' Class 2-6-2T no. 34, which was constructed at Derby Works in 1931 as LMS no. 15534, hauls an up parcels train at Cricklewood. The locomotive was one of the first 40 to be completed and many of these were fitted with condensing apparatus for working in the tunnels of the Metropolitan Widened Lines. As BR no. 40034, the engine was withdrawn during August 1961 after 30 years working from Kentish Town depot.

Cricklewood M7203

This ex-Midland Railway Johnson 2441 Class 0-6-0T is working a local freight train near Cricklewood on 25 June 1948. Built by Vulcan Foundry in July 1901 as MR no. 2444, the engine was renumbered in 1907 to no. 1903 and again in the mid-1930s to 7203; here the locomotive has the 'M' prefix briefly used for ex-LMS stock after 1948.

Cricklewood Station 45536

The 07.25 from Manchester Central travels through Cricklewood behind rebuilt 'Patriot' Class 4-6-0 no. 45536 *Private W. Wood, V.C.* Cricklewood shed and the extensive Brent Empty Wagon Sidings were located on the left of this view, while the Loaded Sidings and Carriage Sidings were on the right behind the express. The locomotive was erected in May 1933 and was named by the hero, who worked on the railways, in 1936.

Croydon 31786
Maunsell L1 4-4-0 no. 31786 is on the line from West Croydon with a breakdown crane, which is perhaps the 45-ton example allocated to Nine Elms shed. The scene has been photographed from a passing Victoria–Brighton line train south of Selhurst station (near Gloucester Road, where the Oliver Typewriter factory was located) on 18 June 1961.

Dudden Hill 33018
Bulleid Q1 Class 0-6-0 no. 33018 travels south with a freight train from Brent Sidings on the former North & South Western Junction Railway line near Acton Wells Junction, Dudden Hill, on 23 April 1955. This freight route was opened in 1853 between Willesden Junction and Kew Junction and remains operational at present.

Above: **Enfield Town Station 69660**

Enfield Town station was the terminus of an intensive suburban service not electrified until November 1960. Two Hill/Gresley N7 Class 0-6-2Ts normally employed on the route are seen: no. 69660 on the right and no. 69671 rests to the left. Hill's design was adopted as a Group Standard Class after Grouping and the two locomotives were built as part of 20 ordered from Robert Stephenson & Co. No. 69660 entered service in November 1925, while no. 69671 was the last of the batch to be completed in January 1926. The former was an early casualty before electrification in May 1959 but the latter remained in employment until steam traction ceased to run in the area from 9 September 1962.

Opposite page, from top to bottom:

East Acton Station 3814

On 23 July 1949, down empty milk wagons pass East Acton LPTB station behind Collett 2884 Class 2-8-0 no. 3814. The train is probably the afternoon Class D Wood Lane–Plymouth milk empties; the corresponding full tankers having come up from Penzance overnight—a service which operated seven days a week. No. 3814 is heading the train on the Ealing & Shepherd's Bush line opened by the Great Western Railway in 1917, mainly for freight movements, from the West London Line at Viaduct Junction. In 1920 East Acton station opened to accommodate passenger trains of the Central London Railway, later Central Line. During the late 1930s the number of tracks used on the route was increased to four in order to separate freight and passenger movements.

Euston Station 46228

At the end of platform 13, Stanier 'Coronation' Class 4-6-2 no. 46228 *Duchess of Rutland* is about to leave on the 10.25 service to Carlisle and Windermere. Ahead is the Ampthill Square bridge no. 2. Until 1952 there would also have been the bridge no. 1, making the whole top end of the station very restricted, also being dominated by no. 2 signal box. No. 2 bridge would be removed when the new Euston station was built.

Above: **Euston Station 45292**
Stanier 5MT or 'Black Five' 4-6-0 no. 45292 looks quite out of place at Euston station in this picture taken from the end of the arrival platforms, looking back towards the station, in July 1965. The 'modern' station building is progressing rapidly and the overhead wires are in place ready for the first electric train to run in November 1965.

Opposite page, from top to bottom:

Euston Station
The remains of Euston Hotel feature in this view north towards the Euston station building site, captured during September 1963. The famous Doric Portico (more correctly a propylaea), which was situated between the station and the hotel on the road from Euston Road/Euston Square, had long since been consigned to a watery grave in one of the biggest outrages of the era. Two hotels were completed initially in 1839, to the design of Philip Hardwick, just after the opening of the station by the London & Birmingham Railway in 1837. These were on the eastern and western sides of Euston Place (just south of the station), but from the early 1880s they were linked by a new hotel built across the approach road. This building is seen here in the final stage of demolition and the site has since been utilised for Euston bus station and office blocks.

Euston Station
The construction site of the new station is seen in late 1963 from the ticket barrier end of the arrival platform side. The enlargement of Euston station had been under consideration for many years prior to the BR Modernisation Plan of 1955. As part of the West Coast Main Line Electrification the decision was finally made to erect a new station. Taylor Woodrow Construction were awarded the contract for the job in 1961, with BRs' London Midland Region architect R. L. Moorcroft working in tandem with Richard Seifert & Partners on the design. The first phase of the project saw work on the lines and platforms completed; these latter were increased in length to the south and their number rose from 15 to 18. As part of the second phase a new concourse, office blocks for BR staff and a multi-storey car park were completed. The new Euston station was opened by H.M. the Queen on 14 October 1968.

Euston Station 42367

Euston station on 6 April 1962, just before reconstruction had claimed the train shed. Departure platforms 14 and 15 feature (on the west side of the site), with Fowler 4P 2-6- 4T no. 42367 in charge of empty stock brought in from Willesden for a down express.

Euston Station Hotel and Approach

Looking north from Euston Road to the thoroughfare installed in the early 1870s to improve access to the station. The bronze of Robert Stephenson, Engineer of the L&BR, was erected at this time as were the two lodges (only one is visible). The London & North Western Railway war memorial was a later addition, but the latter two features are still in their original locations. The statue, by Carlo Marochetti, has been removed to a position outside the station entrance.

Feltham 30839

An up freight approaches Feltham marshalling yard behind Maunsell S15 Class 4-6-0 no. 30839 on 1 April 1958. Urie had originally produced the design for the L&SWR, but after Grouping Maunsell made some modifications and had 45 more erected. No. 30839 was part of the final batch of ten and entered traffic from Eastleigh in May 1936.

Feltham Shed 33016

Q1 no. 33016 had a long-term allocation to Feltham depot from October 1954 to December 1962. Three Bridges had no. 33016 afterwards and withdrawal occurred there the following September. The engine is between duties at Feltham shed on 11 May 1959.

Above: **Feltham Marshalling Yard 30493**

One of the largest marshalling yards in the country, Feltham was purpose-built by the L&SWR in the early 1920s to handle almost all the company's freight traffic to and through London. At the height of operations about 5,500 wagons per day were processed and approx. 150 trains entered and exited with freight services. This picture, captured 1 April 1958, shows Urie G16 Class 4-8-0T no. 30493 working in the down yard and passing Feltham East signal box; the main line was to the left of this, as were the up reception sidings. With the reduction of freight traffic in the 1950s and 1960s, the complex fell out of use and had been swept away by January 1969, later becoming a nature reserve. No. 30493 was built in July 1921 and lasted until December 1959.

Opposite page, from top to bottom:

Feltham Shed 30355

Ex-L&SWR Drummond 700 Class 0-6-0 no. 30355 was built at Dübs & Co. during June 1897 as no. 714. However, this was changed a short time later in May 1898 to no. 355. The locomotive was altered further through the addition of a superheater in July 1929, being the last of the class to receive the component. No. 30355 was withdrawn from Feltham in February 1961 after nearly ten years at the depot.

Feltham Marshalling Yard 30494

Urie's G16 Class engines were constructed specifically for the task of shunting wagons in the yards at Feltham. Four were built at Eastleigh Works in 1921, no. 30494 being completed in August. The design was based on the L&SWR's S15 Class 4-6-0s, but there were a number of differences. The driving wheels of the G16s were 6 in. smaller at 5 ft 1 in., while the cylinders were an inch larger at 22 in. The tractive effort was also higher for the G16s at 33,991 than the 28,200 lb of the S15 Class. No. 30494 is seen in the yard on 11 May 1959 and would remain at work there until withdrawn in December 1962.

Above: **Fenchurch Street Station E8619**

The Railway Correspondence and Travel Society's East London Tour of 14 April 1951 employed Holden J69 Class no. E8619, Hill J19 Class no. 64647 and Fowler 3F 0-6- 0T no. 47300. No. E8619 worked the Fenchurch Street to North Woolwich section, being pictured at the former, then on to Stepney East. Other places taken in by the tour included: Canning Town, Stratford, Bromley, East Ham and Woodgrange Park; the jaunt concluded at Stratford. E8619 had recently been chosen to be the Liverpool Street station pilot and for the task was specially painted in apple green livery with lining, also being given the temporary 'E' prefix and 'British Railways' lettering on the tank sides.

Opposite page, from top to bottom:

Feltham Shed 139

Dugald Drummond became Locomotive Engineer (later styled Chief Mechanical Engineer) of the L&SWR in 1895 and remained in the position until his death in 1912. During this time he produced several large and related locomotive classes for the company, one being the K10 4-4-0s for mixed traffic duties. No. 139 was built at Nine Elms Works in October 1902 as part of order no. A11. The locomotive was withdrawn in September 1948, a year after being photographed at Feltham on 27 September 1947.

Feltham Shed 834

On the south side of Feltham shed in 1947 are two of the Maunsell S15 Class 4-6-0s. Many of these were used for the main line freight workings from Feltham Yard and at the start of 1947, 31 were rostered for the depot's duties. The front locomotive is no. 834 (built November 1927, withdrawn November 1964), while behind is no. 837 (constructed January 1928 and condemned in September 1965); both ended their careers at Feltham. The depot was built as part of the marshalling yard works and came into operation around the time of Grouping. Feltham had six roads, a 65 ft turntable, 200-ton mechanical coaler and repair shop (seen behind the engines) with 50-ton crane.

Above: **Finchley Road 64233**

Gresley J6 0-6-0 no. 64233 (built for the GNR in August 1914) travels along the North London Line (previously NLR) between Finchley Road & Frognal station and West End Lane station (later West Hampstead), and over the former MR line in and out of St Pancras. The locomotive has been photographed on 1 November 1958 from the useful path, recently named Billy Fury Way, running parallel to the line between Finchley Road and West End Lane. No. 64233 was allocated to Hornsey at this time and had been at work from the shed since October 1953. In February 1960 the engine moved on to Peterborough New England and would be condemned there during July 1961.

Opposite page, below:

Finsbury Park Station 2512

Gresley A4 Class Pacific no. 2512 *Silver Fox* is at the head of a stopping-train from Cambridge to King's Cross on 5 June 1946. The engine was quite fresh from a general overhaul and, despite still having wartime black livery applied, the transfers on the tender had reverted back to 'LNER' instead of 'NE'. The locomotive would soon be renumbered 17 in September as part of the 1946 scheme; no. 583 had been allocated originally before the numbers 1-34 were chosen for the class. *Silver Fox* had to wait another 15 months for another general repair to restore the Garter Blue livery and the locomotive also acquired steel cut-out numbers and lettering during this process.

Above: **Finsbury Park Station 2825**

Working the 13.49 Cambridge to King's Cross stopping train—two days prior to *Silver Fox*—is Ivatt C1 Class Atlantic no. 2825. This 1946 number had been on the locomotive since January, replacing 3297 which was used from July 1925, but was applied only briefly as no. 2825 was sent for scrap in February 1947 after 42 years in service.

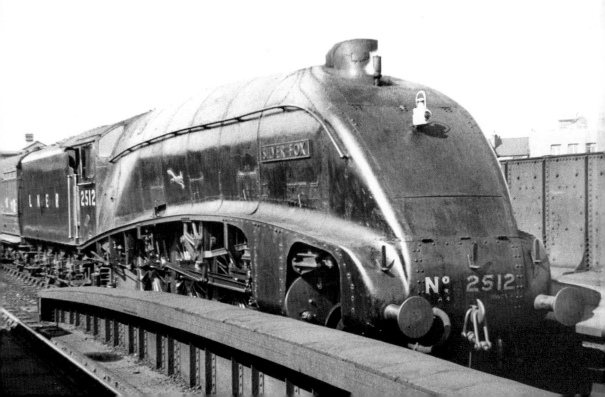

Finsbury Park Station 60122

The Great Northern Railway completed the first section of their line between Maiden Lane, near King's Cross, and Peterborough in August 1850. Despite running through Finsbury Park, a station was not given Board approval until the end of 1860. The opening occurred the following year; the name being Seven Sisters Road until 1869. As built the station only had two wooden platforms, but these were replaced by islands when the Edgware, Highgate & London Railway came close to completion in the late 1860s. Finsbury Park was also later connected with the NLR via Canonbury Junction; No. 3 signal box, seen behind the train, controlled the down line, in addition to the exits from Clarence Yard and the goods and coal depot. Running through Finsbury Park on the down fast is the 10.20 express from King's Cross to Leeds, Bradford and Halifax, which is behind Peppercorn A1 Class Pacific no. 60122 *Curlew* (built December 1948, withdrawn December 1962).

Above: **Hadley Wood 92149**

On 17 March 1962, BR Standard Class 9F 2-10-0 no. 92149 takes a train of empty wagons (of the 16-ton steel variety) northward on the new down slow line and is approaching the former site of Greenwood signal box. The section of line between New Barnet and Potters Bar had only been widened in 1959 to help ease congestion on this former two-line segment of the route. No. 92149 was one of nine class members, from ten built for the Eastern Region, allocated to Peterborough in 1957 after their completion at Crewe Works. The locomotive was based there from October 1957 until withdrawn in June 1965 and would have primarily been employed on coal train duties between the marshalling yards at Peterborough New England and Ferme Park.

Opposite page, below: **Hadley Wood 60149**

A King's Cross express service to Leeds and Bradford is again featured, but the train is the later 13.20 and the locomotive is Peppercorn A1 Pacific no. 60149 *Amadis*. The location is also further north at Hadley Wood, looking south from Monken Hadley Common towards New Barnet station. A total of 49 Pacifics were built to A. H. Peppercorn's design in 1948 and 1949, with no. 60149 being one of 23 erected at Darlington Works. The locomotive entered traffic in May 1949 to Grantham and worked on and off from the shed until September 1956 when a move to King's Cross occurred. By the time *Amadis* was pictured here on 17 March 1962, several years had been spent working from Doncaster. The engine was condemned there in June 1964.

Hadley Wood 60107

Gresley A3 Class Pacific no. 60107 *Royal Lancer* was built at Doncaster in May 1923 as A1 Class no. 1476. The engine was rebuilt to A3 specifications in October 1946, acquiring the diagram 94A boiler, and has also received a Kylchap double chimney and blastpipe along with smoke deflectors, fitted in June 1959 and February 1962 respectively. *Royal Lancer* is travelling northward on the down fast line with the 13.00 King's Cross to Newcastle on 17 March 1962.

Harringay West Station 1809

No. 1809, of Gresley's K3 Class, was the final engine of the first ten to be built by the GNR in August 1921. Originally, no. 1809 (from September 1925) was numbered 4009 and was classified H4 by the company. The locomotive is seen just south of Harringay West station, running tender-first towards Finsbury Park, on 12 April 1947.

Harringay West Station 60055

The 08.47 Hull to King's Cross is hauled through Harringay West by A3 no. 60055 *Woolwinder* at the end of February 1960. The engine received a double chimney in June 1958 and was the first to be altered in the late 1950s. No. 60055 was also one of several A3s to have the 'wing' type smoke deflectors before the adoption of the 'trough' type.

Harringay West Station 8774

Shunting from Ferme Park marshalling yard's up sidings on 12 April 1947 is Stirling/ Ivatt J52 0-6-0ST no. 8774; behind the engine is the south end of the Ferme Park flyover. The locomotive was one of many class members to be allocated to Hornsey for working in the yard and on transfer freights around the London area.

Above: **Harringay West Station 92174**

Before all the traffic was lost to road hauliers, an accelerated fish service from Aberdeen, Hull, Grimsby, etc. to London was provided by the Eastern Region and employed new vacuum-fitted insulated vans designated 'Blue Spot'. Here, empty vans are being worked north, taking the down fast line through Harringay West station, on 3 April 1958. Forging ahead with the service is BR 9F no. 92174, which was allocated to Doncaster for the seven years (February 1958 to December 1965) the engine spent in traffic.

Above: **Harringay West Station 69536**

Like Finsbury Park station, Harringay was a later addition to the GNR main line. The station was one of two opened for suburban traffic on 1 May 1885, the other being Hadley Wood. Harringay was built at the request of British Land Co., which constructed a number of properties in the area, and was also partially funded by the company to the amount of approx. £4,000. On 18 June 1951 the station became Harringay West and this remained in use until 27 May 1971 when the name reverted to the original. N2/2 no. 69536 (built May 1924 as no. 4757, withdrawn in June 1959) is in charge of two Gresley quad-articulated sets for a Hatfield service on 3 April 1958.

Opposite page, below:

Harringay West Station 68903

No. 68903 was built at Doncaster in February 1915 for work in the West Riding of Yorkshire, with the design, classified J23 by the GNR, being tailored to suit the area's steep inclines. A total of 30 were built before Grouping, at which time Gresley developed the design to form Group Standard Class J50. The J23s were reclassified J51 in 1923, but they were rebuilt with slightly larger boilers between 1929 and 1935, becoming J50s. No. 68903 was rebuilt in April 1932. The class were mostly confined to the north of England until before the Second World War when several were sent to Hatfield, Hornsey and King's Cross. They returned north after the onset of the conflict, but a mass influx occurred in 1952 when 30 arrived at Hornsey to take up some of the shed's freight duties. No. 68903 appeared from Ardsley in November and remained employed until withdrawn in April 1961.

Hatch End 45674

The 15.45 Euston to Manchester London Road is about to pass under Little Oxhey Lane, Hatch End, on 13 July 1957 with Stanier 'Jubilee' no. 45674 *Duncan* in charge. Built in 1936, this engine was a regular at Crewe North post-war and lasted until October 1964.

Hatch End 45635

View south from the Cattle Bridge north of Hatch End station. A relief to Manchester is on the down fast from Euston and is headed by 'Jubilee' no. 45635 *Tobago*—a Newton Heath locomotive, which survived until September 1964.

Hendon Station 42846

Hendon station was opened by the MR on 13 July 1868 as the company extended their line from Bedford to St Pancras. Burton-on-Trent-allocated Hughes 5P4F 'Crab' Class 2-6-0 no. 42846 passes through Hendon on 30 September 1949 with an express freight service. The locomotive had been working from the shed since August 1937 and would continue to do so until a move to Cricklewood occurred in February 1954.

Hither Green Shed 31298

C Class no. 31298 is at the entry point to Hither Green shed, with the loop line to Lee on the right. To the rear is the depot's ramped coal stage, installed upon opening in 1933.

Holborn Viaduct Station (Approaches)

Ludgate Hill station (closed since 2 March 1929) provides the vantage point for a view of the approach lines to Holborn Viaduct station, which is ahead in the distance and the Metropolitan Widened Lines (left). Holborn Viaduct (High Level) station was opened by the LC&DR on 2 March 1874 as the final act of the City Line extension project from Herne Hill to Farringdon. The route had reached Blackfriars Bridge in June 1864, Ludgate Hill in December 1864 and through Snow Hill to Farringdon in January 1866, thus allowing trains to transfer north/south through central London.

King's Cross Station 69568

Gresley N2/4 no. 69568 (erected October 1928, withdrawn September 1962) moves vans from platform one across the arrival lines on 24 April 1948. The locomotive was a long-term servant of King's Cross shed and was one of 58 of the class based there.

King's Cross Station 60067
Gresley A3 no. 60067 Ladas makes an impressive display of starting a relief express to York and Hull on 3 April 1958. The engine was Doncaster-based at this time, but would spend three years at King's Cross 'Top' shed before withdrawal in December 1962.

King's Cross Station 35017
Bulleid 'Merchant Navy' Class Pacific no. 35017 *Belgian Marine* takes charge of the 13.10 to Leeds during the locomotive interchange trials performed by BR after Nationalisation in 1948. The engine, and class mates, were acquitted well against their competitors, but were found lacking in some areas. An LMS 4,000 gallon tender has been fitted so water could be collected from the troughs along the route.

King's Cross Station 60503

King's Cross was the preferred site for the terminus of the London & York Railway, later GNR, when the scheme was proposed in the mid-1840s. But, as the works progressed in the latter half of the decade, there was an attempt by some board members to move the site of the terminus north of Regent's Canal to reduce costs. In the event, the line's engineers, William Cubitt and his son Joseph, along with other members of the board, pressed ahead with the plans and the station was ready for traffic on 14 October 1852, although the occasion passed without ceremony. Interestingly, the temporary terminus at Maiden Lane, which had been in use since the line opened on 7 August 1850, was referred to as King's Cross by the GNR. The erection of the permanent station, by John Jay to the design of Lewis Cubitt, did not begin until April 1851 as a hospital had to be demolished, but afterwards progress was quite swift. As completed, and remaining in much the same condition now, the two train sheds were (each) 71 ft high, 800 ft long and 105 ft wide. There were two platforms; one for arrivals on the eastern side and one for departures on the western side. The space between was used for storing carriages. The total cost for the building work was £123,500 and about half of the sum had been spent on purchasing the land. In 1863 York Road platform was opened as the Metropolitan Railway began services to King's Cross and during 1875 two platforms were added to host GNR suburban services. At platform seven with the 17.05 to Newcastle on 25 May 1958 is Thompson A2/2 Class Pacific no. 60503 *Lord President*.

King's Cross Station 60125 and 61179

Passengers on platform four alight from an express from Grimsby, which has been brought to the capital behind Thompson B1 Class 4-6-0 no. 61179. The main aim of Edward Thompson, upon succeeding Sir Nigel Gresley as Chief Mechanical Engineer of the LNER in 1941, was to standardise the company's motive power as far as possible. As he only spent five years in office this plan did not come fully to fruition, but the B1 Class were perhaps the most successful of the designs that were produced during this period. A total of 410 were constructed between 1942 and 1950, with no. 61179 entering traffic from Vulcan Foundry in June 1947. After being run-in at Gorton shed, the locomotive spent just over 11 years at Sheffield before being transferred to King's Cross. When the latter shed closed to steam in June 1963, no. 61179 went north to Doncaster and a year later moved to Immingham, where withdrawal occurred in January 1965. On the left, at platform five with an unidentified express, is Peppercorn A1 Pacific no. 60125 *Scottish Union*. The locomotive followed in the tradition of naming Doncaster Pacifics after racehorses, with 'Scottish Union' being the winner of the St Leger in 1938. Several members of the class were similarly named, while others took the names displaced from renamed or withdrawn locomotives, Locomotive Superintendents of the GNR and NER and constituent companies of the LNER. Only one A1 was to be named originally, no. 60114 *W. P. Allen*, but this decision was soon overturned and the process took place between April 1950 and July 1952. No. 60125 was named during January 1951.

King's Cross Station 22

No. 22 *Mallard* has been pictured in the 'bottom' locomotive yard at King's Cross on 5 May 1948. The engine had been specially selected, along with three other A4s, to participate in the 1948 locomotive exchanges. *Mallard* was to perform the tests in the Western Region from 3 May, but 'ran hot' the week before and was replaced by no. 60033 *Seagull*.

King's Cross Station 69824

Robinson A5/1 Class 4-6-2T no. 69824 is seen in April 1958 when the engine spent a very brief period on trial at King's Cross. The authorities hoped that no. 69824 would fare better than L1 Class 2-6-4Ts when moving the heavy sleeping car trains out of the station, but this was not the case and the locomotive was sent back to Grantham.

Liverpool Street Station Entrance, July 1955

At the end of 1873 building work for the GER's Liverpool Street station finally began after financial difficulties stalled the project. The work was completed in November 1875 and cost £131,911. The entrance is seen in July 1955, with the station hotel on the right. This opened in May 1884 and was designed by Charles Barry and his eldest son in the North Italian Renaissance style with Gothic additions.

Liverpool Street Station 1516

View north from platform nine as B12/3 no. 1516 has the smokebox cleared. As LNER no. 8516 this engine was built in November 1913, rebuilt to B12/3 in November 1932 and withdrawn during July 1958. On the right is the cab approach road off Pindar Street and to the left is an unidentified B1 4-6-0.

Above: **Liverpool Street Station 70007**
When the principal express services from Liverpool Street to East Anglia were increased in frequency during the early 1950s the new BR Standard Class 7 'Britannia' Pacifics were rostered to head the trains. Class member no. 70007 *Coeur de Lion* (built in April 1951) spent ten years working the services from Norwich and is checked over before returning on 17 November 1960. The engine was condemned in June 1965.

Opposite page, from top to bottom:

Liverpool Street Station West Side
As built the station consisted of ten platforms, of which eight were for suburban traffic and two were for main line trains. The eastern section was added later in 1894 and brought the number of platforms in use to 18. Liverpool Street's western side platforms one to five feature in this typical scene at the station, captured on 14 December 1957. The inner suburban services were handled in this part of the site and the platforms were 550 ft long, whereas the two original main line platforms were longer by 450 ft.

Liverpool Street Station 1580
S. D. Holden designed the GER Class S69 (LNER B12/1) locomotives for the heavier trains abounding on the company's main line just after the turn of the twentieth century. Seventy engines were built before Grouping, while a further ten were built in 1928 to relieve a motive power crisis during the design stage for a new class to handle the express traffic. Entering service in October, no. 1580 was the last of this final batch. The locomotive is backing out of platform nine, under Pindar Street bridge on 28 April 1947.

Above: Liverpool Street Station 69614

Fairbairn Engineering Co. was responsible for the 1875 train-shed's ironwork and roof, which consisted of four spans. Two central spans 109 ft wide were flanked by two smaller ones, of approximately 45 ft. The former were supported by pairs of wrought iron columns decorated with cast iron and these are seen behind N7/4 Class 0-6-2T no. 69614, an early N7, no. 7991 of December 1923. The locomotive was the west side station pilot and, like J69 no. 68619 working on the east side, was specially embellished for the duty.

Opposite page, from top to bottom:

Liverpool Street Station 70007 and 61880

No. 70007 *Coeur de Lion* has also been photographed in August 1958. The engine's location is Liverpool Street's locomotive yard as viewed from the cab road off Primrose Street. On the right, at platform ten, is Gresley K3 Class 2-6-0 no. 61880 (constructed in October 1929 as no. 1387, withdrawn September 1962), which is in charge of an up express. Liverpool Street station saw large-scale modernisation work between 1982 and 1991 as the site was rationalised and improved. The area of the station depicted, and much northward, was covered over and building developments placed above.

London Bridge Station 42069

Fairburn Class 4MT 2-6-4T no. 42069 was built at Brighton Works October 1950 and allocated to Ramsgate for the first year in service. Spells at Ashford and Three Bridges followed before no. 42069 moved to the LMR in December 1959. Here, the engine is at London Bridge station's platform 17 with the 18.15 train to Tunbridge Wells West on 30 April 1959.

London Bridge Station 30534

View eastward from the platform ends of the ex-LB&SCR station towards the London suburbs and Kent, with the station's large signal box in the background. Maunsell Q Class 0-6-0 no. 30534 (built in August 1938 and withdrawn during August 1962) is from Tunbridge Wells West and engaged on the non-electrified Oxted line services.

London Bridge Station 47642

Heading an inter-regional freight train from Hither Green marshalling yard to the LMR's Brent marshalling yard is Fowler Class 3F 0-6-0T no. 47642. The engine will travel via Blackfriars Bridge and the ex-Metropolitan Widened Lines to connect with the ex-MR main line at St Paul's Road Junction north of St Pancras.

London Bridge Station 1706

The 'Low Level' (un-roofed) platforms, nos 8-10, formed the original terminus of the L&GR and L&CR, opened between 1836–39. Above and to the right are platforms 1–7 of the SER through lines to Cannon Street and Charing Cross. A relic from LC&DR days is Kirtley R1 Class 0-4-4T no. 1706, which is at work on station pilot duties.

London Bridge Station 30806

Maunsell N15 'King Arthur' Class no. 30806 *Sir Galleron* is running light engine up the Eastern Section through line to take an express from one of the termini on 22 July 1949. The locomotive was the last to be built at Eastleigh Works in January 1927 and was withdrawn in April 1961. To the right, at platform four, is a suburban EMU.

Above: **London Bridge Station 30925**

Maunsell 'Schools' Class 4-4-0 no. 30925 *Cheltenham* is moments away from departure with the RCTS 'Sussex Rail Tour' on 7 October 1962. No. 30925 went as far as Brighton, where no. 32636 and 32418 took over to Seaford, Newhaven and then back to Brighton. No. 32353 then returned the party to London Bridge. *Cheltenham* would be withdrawn soon after the tour in December 1962, but the locomotive was selected to be a part of the National Collection and, after 33 years at the National Railway Museum, has recently been restored and is at work on the Mid-Hants Railway or 'Watercress line'.

Opposite page, from top to bottom:

London Bridge Station 31865

No. 31865 was built at Ashford Works during June 1925 and, as was the case with nearly all the N Class, was fitted with a top feed and smokebox-mounted regulator. In the 1930s ten were built with regulators in the dome and the decision was made subsequently that the other Ns should conform in this respect. Smoke deflectors were also being fitted during this period and the class were again modified. No. 31865 differs in another aspect as a BR Standard Class 4 chimney and arrangement has been acquired at some point after 1957. The locomotive was a long-term Redhill resident and was condemned at the shed in September 1963.

London Bridge Station 34016

Bulleid 'Light' Pacific no. 34016 *Bodmin* has been preserved since being withdrawn in October 1966. The engine was taken from Barry scrapyard and spent time at the Mid-Hants Railway before recently heading north to Carnforth for an overhaul in readiness for a return to steam. *Bodmin* is still very much hard at work in this photograph, captured on 30 April 1959, as the engine hauls the 15.25 from Margate, via Dover and Ashford, to Charing Cross station past platform seven at London Bridge.

Above: **London Bridge Station 80034**

At the buffer stops at London Bridge station on 7 October 1962 is BR Standard Class 4 2-6-4T no. 80034. The Southern Region was in need of locomotives for secondary passenger duties after Nationalisation and, after the success of LMS Fairburn 2-6-4-Ts, Brighton drawing office produced a design based on the former class. No. 80034 was erected at Brighton in April 1952, but went to the LMR until December 1959 when allocated to Ashford. The engine had moved on to Stewarts Lane by May 1962 and would have spells at Brighton, Redhill and Feltham before withdrawal in January 1966.

Opposite page, from top to bottom:

London Bridge Station 75070

BR Standard Class 4 4-6-0s also shared a lineage with the Class 4 2-6-4T and were produced for a similar reason, only their main sphere of activity was to be the Western Region. The SR was allocated 15 of the 80 built, these being nos 75065–75079. No. 75070, which is being admired at London Bridge before taking out the 16.40 to East Grinstead via Oxted on 24 April 1959, was built in October 1955 and working from Brighton when pictured, despite the engine still displaying the 71A code for Eastleigh.

London Bridge Station 32326

LB&SCR L. B. Billinton J2 Class 4-6-2T no. 32326 departs with the 16.40 service to Uckfield on 30 September 1948. Only two of the 'J' design were completed; D. E. Marsh designed the first, a J1, before Billinton succeeded him and modified some details. No. 326 *Bessborough* was built at Brighton in March 1912 and was in service to June 1951. Originally working the company's principal expresses, by 1946 the J Class were allocated to Tunbridge Wells West for the shed's express duties to and from Victoria and London Bridge. Both engines were specially painted in Malachite green for these tasks, but no. 32326 was unique in having 'British Railways' applied to the tank-sides.

London Bridge Station

At platform two with the 14.25 express from Charing Cross to Hastings is 'Schools' Class locomotive no. 30936 *Cranleigh*. The Hastings route featured a number of poorly constructed tunnels which restricted the line's loading gauge. This was taken into account when the class was designed and resulted in the adoption of a round-top boiler and small cab. The coaching stock used on the route was also necessarily modified.

Loughton Station

Pictured, on 9 March 1957, is the third station to serve Loughton. In preparation for the takeover of the line by London Transport a new station was built to the design of John Murray Easton and Robertson Fellows. This Loughton station was open from 28 April 1940, but Central Line services did not start until 21 November 1947. The station has since been listed Grade II.

Marylebone Station 60063

Marylebone station was ready for traffic on 15 March 1899 after the GCR extended their line from Nottingham to London. Only four platforms were used; two for arrivals and two for departures. A3 Class no. 60063 *Isinglass* is seen on platform four in mid-May 1956 with the 10.00 service to Manchester London Road via Sheffield Victoria.

Marylebone Station 45253

Stanier 'Black Five' 4-6-0 no. 45253 was a disappointment in the locomotive exchanges, especially on the ex-GC line despite the best efforts of the crew. No. 45253 is recorded here entering Marylebone with the 08.25 express from Manchester on 16 June 1948; on the previous day's run the engine had arrived 34 minutes late. Note the three other photographers recording the return; two are on the signal gantry.

Marylebone Station 6990

On 25 June 1948 Hawksworth 'Modified Hall' Class 4-6-0 no. 6990 *Witherslack Hall* arrives at Marylebone with the same service as no. 45253. The locomotive performed little better than the latter, averaging 3.84 lb of coal per drawbar horsepower hour compared to the 3.29 lb and 3.32 lb of the 'Black Five' and B1 respectively. The locomotive was relatively new at this time, having emerged from Swindon Works in April 1948. No. 6990 would continue in service until December 1965 and has since been preserved, presently residing at the GCR, Loughborough.

Marylebone Station 34006

The Bulleid Pacifics were modified in order to take part in the locomotive exchanges, including being fitted with: speed recorders, extended smoke deflectors and v-shaped cab fronts. No. 34006 *Bude* was in Brighton Works for nearly seven weeks before taking part on the Marylebone to Manchester services between 7 and 11 June. The engine handled the trains easily and produced some very impressive drawbar horsepower figures during the week, although the coal consumption was quite high.

North Kent West Junction/Rotherhithe Road Carriage Sidings 34012
Loitering at an imprecise location near North Kent West Junction and Rotherhithe Road carriage sidings on 9 July 1958 was Bulleid 'West Country' Pacific no. 34012 *Launceston*. The locomotive had been rebuilt by BR at the beginning of the year and this was the cheapest transformation during the period, costing £7,646. No. 34012 had also run just over 500,000 miles since being built in October 1945. *Launceston* was allocated to Bricklayers Arms shed from February 1958 to July 1962 and the engine would continue in traffic until December 1966, running a further 346,000 miles (approximate).

North Kent West Junction/Bricklayers Arms Branch 34004
Near to South Bermondsey station on the ex-LB&SCR main line, North Kent West Junction connected the adjacent ex-SE&CR main line to Bricklayers Arms goods depot and the engine sheds. There were also two lines to New Cross Gate, primarily for freight traffic running to the goods yards there. Coming off the Bricklayers Arms Branch is Bulleid 'Light' Pacific no. 34004 *Yeovil*. The bridge behind carried the South London Line.

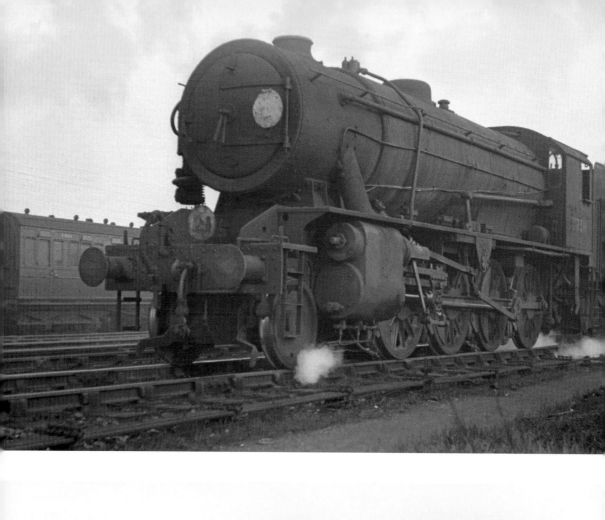

Above: **North Kent West Junction/Bricklayers Arms Branch 32348**
L. B. Billinton K Class 2-6-0 no. 32348 heads west towards Bricklayers Arms depot on 9 July 1958. The
locomotive entered service from Brighton in December 1920 and was fitted with a boiler constructed by Derby
Works. This was because the former was working to capacity and unable to complete the task. The boiler had
two domes and a top feed, but these features were later discarded from the class during the 1930s.

Opposite page, from top to bottom:

North Kent West Junction/Bricklayers Arms Junction 77311
Former LMS Mechanical and Electrical Engineer (Scotland) R. A. Riddles developed W. Stanier's 8F design for
use by the War Department during the Second World War. A total of 935 were built and all but three saw use
in the European theatre. No. 77311 was constructed at the North British Locomotive Company's Queens Park
Works during May 1943 and after returning to England worked for the SR, and later BR, from Bricklayers
Arms. The locomotive, pictured on 31 December 1948 coming off the Bricklayers Arms Branch, later became
no. 90226 in July 1949 and would work on the LMR from May 1951 until withdrawn in December 1963.

North Kent West Junction/Bricklayers Arms Branch 32449
R. Billinton's C2 Class were produced in numbers between 1893 and 1902 when 55 were in service for the
LB&SCR working goods trains. No. 32449 was built in October 1894 at Vulcan Foundry and was later modified
by Marsh to become C2X in January 1912. At Nationalisation the engine was allocated to Horsham, but by
1950 a move to Redhill had occurred. Here, no. 32449, pictured on 9 July 1958, has the 75A shed code, which
signifies a Brighton residency. The locomotive had been there since December 1956 and would remain until
March 1961 when Three Bridges took charge of the engine. No. 32449 was condemned only three months later.

Above: **Neasden South Junction 61063**

A Marylebone to Woodford Halse stopping service leaves the ex-GCR main line at Neasden South Junction to take the ex-GWR and GCR Joint line via High Wycombe. The train, headed by B1 no. 61063, would then rejoin the main line via Ashendon Junction. The route was opened to passengers on 2 April 1906 and consisted of two new sections of tracks between Northolt Junction and High Wycombe and Princes Risborough to Ashendon Junction. The Wycombe Railway line between High Wycombe and Princes Risborough was bought by the Joint Committee and in total the route amounted to nearly 34 miles. This picture dates from 2 May 1959 and empty stock, which had taken passengers to Wembley Stadium for the FA Cup Final, is seen on the right.

Opposite page, below:

Neasden Shed 80137

BR Standard Class 4 2-6-4T no. 80137 was one of the last batch of 24 engines to be built at Brighton Works between 1956 and 1957, being erected in May of the former year. These locomotives were fitted with partial water pick-up apparatus, speedometers and ball-joint superheaters. Initially, the authorities were to allocate nos 80131 to 80144 to Plaistow for the trains running between Fenchurch Street and Tilbury and Fairburn 2-6-4Ts were to be displaced to Neasden. In the event, only Nos 80131 to 80136 were allocated to Plaistow and 80137 to 80144 were sent to Neasden and worked the depot's suburban services. These eight locomotives were swapped from 29 November 1959, in addition to 26 other Standard Class 4s, with 34 SR-allocated Fairburn 2-6-4Ts. No. 80137 was moved to Tunbridge Wells West.

Above: **Neasden Shed 67717**

Neasden depot served the motive power used on the passenger and freight traffic at the London end of the ex-GCR main line into Marylebone. The shed was also responsible for the engines used for the freight services running on the ex-Metropolitan lines. Neasden opened during March 1899 and possessed six roads, ramped coal stage and repair shop. At this time the depot housed 30 locomotives, but by 1947 the complement had reached 86. The 2-6-4Ts were all formerly of the Met., but Thompson's L1 was just permeating their ranks and no. 67717, depicted here on 16 July 1948 leaving the shed, was almost brand-new, being built at Darlington in April. The locomotive was the first of the class to have the BR number applied from new and was one of nine despatched to Neasden in mid-1948. No. 67717 would remain until March 1953 then transferred to Lowestoft.

Above: **New Cross Gate Station 2459**

R. J. Billinton E3 Class 0-6-2T locomotive no. 2459 is seen shunting at New Cross Gate station on 24 March 1948. The first of the class, LB&SCR no. 158 *West Brighton*, was designed by William Stroudley before his death and when Billinton took over a small number of revisions were made before a further 16 were ordered. No. 2459 was erected at Brighton Works in December 1895 as *Warlingham*. The locomotive was later a long-term resident at Bricklayers Arms and would be condemned at the shed in June 1957.

Opposite page, from top to bottom:

Neasden Shed 67781

L1 Class no. 67781 is under preparation for the next duty at Neasden shed on 3 March 1957. Shed staff and footplatemen had to be particularly vigilant for problems arising with the L1 Class as some were prone to worn or heated axle boxes and broken cylinder and smokebox saddle bolts. A number of engines working from Neasden in the 1950s were fitted with cylinder liners or had the boiler pressure lowered in an attempt to alleviate these problems. In addition ten were fitted with manganese steel axle box liners, which improved the situation to a certain extent. No. 67781 had several spells at the depot in the early 1950s, finally leaving in June 1957 for Gorton.

Neasden 61163

B1 Class no. 61163 comes off the High Wycombe line with a train for Nottingham Forest supporters attending the 1959 FA Cup Final against Luton Town. Shortly, the train would be reversed to the Wembley Stadium loop line and then move on to Wembley Stadium station. These two features had been undertaken by the GCR shortly before Grouping and were opened by the LNER on 28 April 1923. No. 61163 was built by Vulcan Foundry in May 1947 and during the following month was allocated to Neasden shed, making the engine no stranger to the area. The locomotive was briefly at Leicester before final allocation to Colwick, lasting from December 1954 until condemned in September 1962. The Wembley station loop was in use until May 1968 and has been superseded by the former Wembley Hill station. Incidentally, Forest won the match 2-1.

New Cross Gate Station 33002

New Cross Gate station was opened by the L&CR, as New Cross, on 5 June 1839, later having 'Gate' added by the SR in June 1923. Bulleid Q1 Class no. 33002 heads a train of bogie stone hopper wagons north on 7 April 1957.

New Southgate 60508

Looking eastward across the east coast main line just north of New Southgate Station and Thompson A2/1 Class Pacific no. 60508 *Duke of Rothesay* has derailed as the result of poor track maintenance. The engine was hauling the 19.50 Edinburgh to King's Cross overnight train and came off the rails at approx. 70 mph after the rear, then the front bogie wheels left the line. No. 60508 became detached from the train and overturned, sliding along the side of the boiler for 100 yards. Fireman Young was killed and driver W. Hoole slightly injured, but the passengers emerged relatively unscathed.

New Southgate Station 92181
Passing under Friern Barnet Lane bridge, on the up fast line behind Standard Class 9F no. 92181, is a partially-fitted coal train. The engine was allocated new to Peterborough New England in November 1957 and weathered the influx of diesels until late 1964 when put into storage in preparation for withdrawal, which occurred in February 1965.

New Southgate 5013
Viewed from Oakleigh Road North on 17 June 1948, after the derailment of no. 60508, Ivatt Class J1 (GNR J21) no. 5013 is on hand to assist with the clear-up, being coupled to an engineer's train. The locomotive was one of three J1s recently transferred to Hitchin and would be condemned there in November 1954 as the last to be scrapped.

Nine Elms Shed 30763

Outside the 'old' shed at Nine Elms is Maunsell 'King Arthur' Class no. 30763 *Sir Bors de Ganis*. The locomotive was the first of the batch ordered from the North British Loco to be completed in May 1925 and between then and September a further 29 were sent south. These engines were given names of lesser known characters in Arthurian legend. No. 30763, pictured on 15 February 1958, was allocated to Nine Elms from September 1957 until withdrawn in October 1960.

Nine Elms Shed 30245

The two engine sheds at Nine Elms, near Vauxhall, were opened in 1885 and 1910 by the L&SWR. The former had 15 tracks, while the newer building had 10, both housing passenger and freight locomotives for Waterloo station and Nine Elms goods depot. Drummond M7 Class 0-4-4T no. 30245 worked from the depot for several years under BR and was preserved after withdrawal in November 1962 as part of the National Collection.

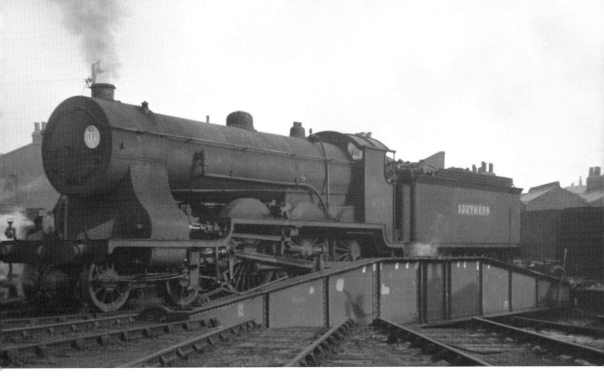

Nine Elms Shed 459

Nine Elms shed's 65 ft turntable was placed in the south-east corner of the depot site, which was located on the southern side of the main line from Waterloo. Being moved by the apparatus on 1 March 1947 is Drummond T14 Class no. 459. The locomotive was built in June 1912 and condemned in November 1948. Nine Elms shed was operational until the end of steam in the SR during July 1967 and in 1971 the land was bought for the erection of New Covent Garden Market, which opened in 1974.

Northfields Station

The District Railway opened Northfields station on 16th April 1908 as Northfield Ealing. Northfields and Little Ealing was the title a short time later before just Northfields was adopted in May 1932. At this time the station was rebuilt, to the design of Charles Holden, for the start of Piccadilly Line services on the Houslow West branch.

Northwick Park E1298

Thompson B1 Class no. E1298 heads north on the Metropolitan Line, near the point where the route crosses over the WCML at Northwick Park, with the 15.20 express from Marylebone to Manchester on 8 May 1948. The engine was a recent addition to stock in March, having arrived at Leicester from the North British Loco. Fifteen other B1s built by the company at this time had the 'E' prefix applied when they were sent into service.

Norwood Junction Station 32413

Resting just north of Norwood Junction station, on 2 April 1958, is R. Billinton E6 Class 0-6-2T no. 32413, which would only remain active for a further seven months. The locomotive had been built at Brighton Works in July 1905 as no. 413 *Fenchurch*.

Norwood Junction 31825

N Class no. 31825 is on the down slow line with a coal train on 2 April 1958. The engine was constructed at Ashford Works in December 1923 and allocated to Bricklayers Arms. Ten years later the locomotive was housed at Ashford, but by Nationalisation no. 31825 had returned to the former and remained at the depot until July 1962.

Norwood Junction Shed 32547

No. 32547, seen here on 2 April 1958, was erected as C2 Class no. 547 in January 1902, then rebuilt during October 1908 and survived until November 1961. The locomotive was one of the few R. Billinton C2X Class 0-6-0s that did not have a double-dome boiler.

Above: **Norwood Junction Shed 31918**

Maunsell W Class 2-6-4T no. 31918 has been pictured in Norwood Junction depot's yard on 12 March 1960. The class were built for working freight services between the marshalling yards in the London area. Two batches were erected at Ashford Works during the first half of the 1930s; no. 31918 was produced as part of the second in June 1935. Also installed at this time was Norwood shed, which was primarily for locomotives working in the nearby goods yards. Five tracks were covered by a northlight roof and the building was fabricated from pre-cast concrete.

Above: **Old Oak Common East Junction 4909**

Empty coaching stock from Old Oak Common carriage sidings is bound for Paddington station behind Collett 'Hall' Class 4-6-0 no. 4909 Blakesley Hall on 11 March 1961. The photograph has been taken from a footbridge off the path beside the Grand Union Canal that led down to the lines and Old Oak Common East Junction signal box. The locomotive was constructed at Swindon in January 1929 and would be withdrawn in September 1962. At this time no. 4909 was allocated to Swindon and had been there for several months after transferring from Exeter. Between November 1957 and November 1961 *Blakesley Hall* was Westbury-allocated.

Opposite page, below:

Old Oak Common Shed 9661

Charles Collett 8750 Class 0-6-0PT no. 9661 is seen in Old Oak Common shed's yard on 2 March 1947. The locomotive had only recently been constructed, being the last of ten engines built to order no. 362 at Swindon Works between November and December 1946; a further ten erected to the order would appear between June and September of the following year. No. 9661 had a long-term allocation to Old Oak Common from new until July 1963 when moved briefly to Wolverhampton Stafford Road, then finally to Oxley where withdrawal occurred in November 1964.

Above: **Old Oak Common East Junction 4975**
'Hall' Class no. 4975 *Umberslade Hall* heads east towards Paddington light engine. The locomotive was one of eighty built to Swindon Lot no. 254 between 1928 and 1930. The class continued to be built in numbers until 1943 when 259 had entered traffic and production of Hawksworth's 'Modified Hall' design began. The bridge carrying the West London Line over the ex-GWR main line can be seen behind no. 4975.

Opposite page, from top to bottom:

Old Oak Common East Junction 1504
Hawksworth's 1500 Class were designed for shunting and had a short wheelbase for this purpose. The ten engines built were also unusual through being fitted with outside cylinders and valve gear. No. 1504 was erected at Swindon in August 1949 and allocated to Old Oak Common until condemned in May 1963. This engine—and several other class mates—were employed at the depot moving the coaching stock to and from Paddington.

Old Oak Common Shed 6013
Collett 'King' Class 4-6-0 no. 6013 *King Henry VIII* is at the front of a line of locomotives resting at Old Oak Common shed on 2 September 1956. The engine had been a recent recipient of a double chimney in June and 12 other 'Kings' would be modified during the year. No. 6013 worked at Old Oak Common until March 1959, then had spells at Plymouth and Wolverhampton before withdrawn in September 1962.

Above: **Old Oak Common East Junction 6169**

Collett's 6100 Class 2-6-2T locomotives were introduced between 1931 and 1935 as a development of his 5100 Class. The former had the boiler pressure increased by 25 psi from the 200 psi of the latter, thereby raising the tractive effort of the 6100 engines to 27,340 lb. This was a 3,040 lb increase on the 5100 Class. No. 6169 was the seventieth and final class member to be built at Swindon Works in November 1935. The locomotive was then allocated to Southall for a lengthy period, but in November 1960 a move to Old Oak Common happened. Travelling to Paddington from the depot on 27 April 1963, no. 6169 would move the following year to Radyr shed in Cardiff. Then, in June 1964 the engine was sent to Worcester where withdrawal would occur during December 1965, the date being also when steam ended in the WR.

Opposite page, below:

Paddington Station 7006

'Castle' Class locomotive no. 7006 *Lydford Castle* is about to depart from platform one at Paddington station on 16 February 1951 with the 16.55 express to Cheltenham St James station; a service popularly known as the 'Cheltenham Flyer'. This had begun in 1932 and was one of the GWR's flagship express trains, lasting well into the post- Nationalisation period. No. 7006 was a late addition to the company's fleet in June 1946 and would remain in traffic until December 1963.

Above: **Old Oak Common Shed with 8763**

The largest shed on the ex-GWR system, Old Oak Common provided almost all of the motive power for the passenger services, and many of the freight trains, operating around London. The facilities were built on the north side of the line from Paddington, just before the tracks split to Wycombe and Reading, and opened during March 1906, consisting of four roundhouses and a repair shop. These were located on the west side of the site and are viewed from the eastern side on 1 September 1956. The large ramped coal stage can be seen on the left, while in the middle distance are the preparation roads; a crane removes some of the ash that has been deposited. Collett 8750 Class 0-6-0PT no. 8763 (June 1933–August 1962) leads a line a goods engines on the right. The locomotive spent a number of years working from Old Oak Common. The depot would remain active until March 1964 when a new diesel shed was built on the land.

Above: **Paddington Concourse**

The GWR's station at Paddington was opened on 4 June 1838, as a provisional terminus on the first section of the London to Bristol main line, which stretched as far as Maidenhead and was 22½ miles long. The new station, east of Bishops Bridge Road, was built to the design of the company's engineer I. K. Brunel and opened in 1854; the departure platforms being ready on 16 January and the arrival platforms on 29 May. Platforms one and two, with the holiday crowds waiting to leave on Saturday, 25 July 1953, are pictured here.

Opposite page, from top to bottom:

Paddington Station 7927 and 5001

Two 4-6-0s have been captured passing underneath Bishops Bridge Road from platform three at Paddington station on 23 May 1958. The engine on the left is 'Castle' Class no. 5001 *Llandovery Castle*, which is departing from platform four with the 18.00 express to Weymouth, while on the right is 'Modified Hall' no. 7927 *Willington Hall*. This locomotive is reversing on to a train at platform three. On the left, empty stock arrives for an early evening train. No. 5001 was allocated to Old Oak Common at this time, whereas no. 7927 was a Reading engine. The latter would survive in service for nearly three years longer than *Llandovery Castle* and after withdrawal in December 1965 the locomotive was prevented from being scrapped and will contribute parts for two new engines now being built to the 'Grange' Class and 'County' Class designs.

Paddington Station 9405

Hawksworth 9400 Class 0-6-0PT no. 9405 was constructed at Swindon in May 1947 as part of the first, and only, batch of the class to be built at the works. A further 200 would be produced after Nationalisation by R. Stephenson & Hawthorns, W. G. Bagnall and Yorkshire Engine Co. No. 9405 is seen moving empty stock at Paddington, only a short time after completion, on 5 July 1947. The locomotive was allocated to Old Oak Common when new and would remain there, with occasional spells at other London Division sheds, until condemned in June 1965.

Paddington Station 6011

The 13.10 express to Birmingham Snow Hill and Wolverhampton Low Level is ready to leave Paddington on 30 May 1960, behind 'King' Class 4-6-0 no. 6011 *King James I*. The locomotive was built at Swindon in April 1928 and was condemned in December 1962. Allocated to Wolverhampton Stafford Road shed when photographed, withdrawal would occur at Old Oak Common.

Paddington Station 8436

Hawksworth 9400 Class 0-6-0PT no. 8436 has transported coaching stock from Old Oak Common to platform four in anticipation of an express passenger service. In London especially, the class were mainly used for empty stock and shunting, but elsewhere some did find use on revenue earning trains. The engine, pictured on 28 June 1962, had only been assigned to Old Oak Common for a month after a number of years in South Wales.

Paddington Station 7001

The 07.30 from Carmarthen finishes the long journey from South-West Wales, pulling in to platform ten at Paddington on 24 April 1948. A recent addition to the complement at Old Oak Common, 'Castle' Class locomotive no. 7001 *Sir James Milne*, which had been in charge of the train from Swansea, is admired by several enthusiasts, both young and old. Only two months previously the engine had been named *Denbigh Castle* (carried since built in May 1946) but, as a way of honouring the last chairman of the GWR, the change had been implemented in February 1948.

Paddington Station 4084

Five years on from the above and the end of platforms ten and eleven is still a popular draw for 'spotters'. The train is now an express from Weston-super-Mare, headed by 'Castle' no. 4084 *Aberystwyth Castle*. On the right is the large Paddington goods station.

Above: **Paddington Station 7000**

Turned out from Swindon in May 1946, 'Castle' Class no. 7000 *Viscount Portal* was the third class member to be built there after the end of the Second World War. Upon the resumption of construction an alteration was made to the design of the boiler. The number of 2 in. diameter tubes was reduced by 17 to 170 and 7 superheater flues were added in their place. Despite not possessing a shed plate in this picture, taken at Paddington on 27 April 1963, *Viscount Portal* had a home at Worcester and arrived a month earlier. Withdrawal would take place in December.

Opposite page, from top to bottom:

Paddington Station 5987

Collett's 'Hall' Class was first introduced in 1924 to improve upon the performance of the mixed traffic 4300 Class 2-6-0. The new class had 6 ft diameter wheels, standard no. 1 boiler and side-window cab. No. 5987 *Brocket Hall*, which is leaving the terminus with the 18.35 relief express to Cheltenham on 23 May 1958, was erected in November 1939 and varied slightly from earlier examples by possessing 9 in. diameter piston valves. The engine was another Old Oak Common resident, but was reaching the end of this allocation as by November the following year Didcot would take possession of no. 5987. In January 1964 *Brocket Hall* was condemned at the shed.

Poplar Station Site

The L&BR opened Poplar station on 6 July 1840 as the penultimate stop on the company's line from Fenchurch Street. The station was moved from the western side of Brunswick Street in 1845 and remained open until 3 May 1926, but the line continued to be used until the mid-1970s. This view was taken looking eastward to the remains of Poplar station on 25 March 1962, with Brunswick Wharf power station in the distance and the lines to the former MR dock heading off on the right.

Purley 31864

Purley station was installed on the London & Brighton line upon opening on 12 July 1841. However, the LB&SCR subsequently closed the facilities, then named Godstone Road, from 1 October 1847. Almost a decade followed before re-opening occurred after the completion of the Caterham line, which joined the main line just south of Purley. The station was renamed Godstone Road Caterham Junction and then just the latter addition for a time before Purley was used from 1 October 1888. Passing through Purley on 3 June 1959 is Maunsell N Class no. 31864.

Queen's Park 3561

Just east of Queen's Park station, no. 3561 travels out to Willesden carriage sidings with a train of empty stock from Euston on the down slow line. The locomotive was built to S. Johnson's design by Sharp, Stewart & Co. in July 1897 for use on MR freight traffic. No. 3561 was employed at Willesden shed when pictured here on 24 April 1948 and would continue in traffic until October 1954, when withdrawn from Rugby.

South Kenton Station 45530

'Patriot' Class 4-6-0 no. 45530 *Sir Frank Ree* speeds past South Kenton station, on the Watford DC Lines, with the 16.30 Euston to Wolverhampton on 8 May 1948. The locomotive began life as a nominal Fowler rebuild from C. B. Cooke's 'Claughton' Class and was later transformed again by W. Stanier in October 1946. No. 45530's name is also not original, formerly belonging to pioneer Fowler rebuild no. 5902 until 1937. *Sir Frank Ree* would be the last of the class to be condemned in December 1965.

Raynes Park Station 34041

A Waterloo to Weymouth relief express passes through Raynes Park station behind Bulleid 'West Country' Pacific no. 34041 *Wilton* on 15 May 1964. The locomotive had been in service since October 1946 and would not be condemned until January 1966. Allocated to Eastleigh for this event, the engine had previously been at Bournemouth.

Above: **Southall Station 9791**

A goods train, attached to Collett '8750' Class no. 9791, joins the GWR main line from the Brentford Dock Branch at Southall station on 28 October 1961. The engine was constructed at Swindon in May 1936 and employed at Southall shed from November 1959 to February 1962. To improve communication between the Thames and the GWR main line, plans were produced, under the guidance of Isambard Kingdom Brunel, for a route from Brentford and the project was authorised in August 1855. Construction of the three miles of track and docks took three years, opening on 18 July 1859. Passenger services were an afterthought and, despite attempts by the GWR to increase usage, these were withdrawn in May 1942. Freight traffic on the line was steady until the early 1960s, when beginning to diminish. The dock closed in 1964 and goods to Brentford ceased in 1970, but the line remains in use for refuse trains.

Opposite page, from top to bottom:

Southall 7018

'Castle' Class 4-6-0 no. 7018 *Drysllwyn Castle* had only a short existence, being built in May 1949 and withdrawn in September 1963. The locomotive heads into London with a parcels train, again, in October 1961.

Southall 92224

Crewe-built 9F no. 92224 would have an even shorter career than no. 7018 thanks to the BR modernisation plan. Erected in June 1958, the locomotive would be condemned for scrap in September 1967. No. 92224, which is in charge of a partially fitted freight travelling on the up relief line, was fitted with a double chimney from new.

Southall 6919

A short distance to the east of Southall station, Collett 'Hall' Class 4-6-0 no. 6919 *Tylney Hall* approaches with a down parcels train. The engine was built during June 1941 and as a result of the war was nameless and without cab windows when entering service. *Tylney Hall* was added in August 1947.

Southall Shed 7923

Outside the west end of Southall shed, on 25 November 1962, is 'Modified Hall' no. 7923 *Speke Hall*. The depot is still in use for preserved locomotives.

St John's Disaster

Dense fog enveloped the evening of 4 December 1957, making sighting signals difficult. Driver Trew was in charge of 'Light' Pacific no. 34066 *Spitfire*, which was at the head of the 16.46 Cannon Street to Dover, when he missed two signals at yellow. The result was a collision with the rear of the 17.18 Charing Cross to Hayes. Ninety people were killed and 108 suffered serious injury. Many of the fatalities were the result of the flyover bridge carrying the Nunhead to Lewisham line collapsing on top of some of the carriages. In this scene gangs of workmen are hard at work removing the bridge.

St Pancras Station 34005

Bulleid 'West Country' Pacific no. 34005 *Barnstaple* arrives at St Pancras with an express from Manchester on 17 June 1948 as part of the locomotive exchanges. Like classmate 34006 *Bude*, the engine's performance outshone the competitors in a number of areas.

St Pancras Station 45614

Only seven months after taking office in January 1932, LMS C. M. E. W. Stanier had his Class 5 express passenger design, or 'Jubilee' Class, authorised for construction as part of the 1934 building programme. No. 45614 *Leeward Islands*, seen here on 18 March 1961 on an express, was one of 48 built at Crewe Works, entering service in August.

St Pancras Station 160 and M161

Two of Stanier's 3P Class 2-6-2T have been caught ready to move empty stock at St Pancras on 10 June 1948. At platform one is no. 160, while at two is M161, both being constructed at Derby in 1937. Cricklewood sidings housed the stock used at St Pancras.

St Pancras Station 73142
The MR opened St Pancras station on 1 October 1868 after the company extended their line from Bedford.
W. H. Barlow was the architect for the station and the single span roof, which crosses a distance of 245 ft.
In this picture, taken on 13 June 1957, shafts of light penetrate the gloom as BR Standard Class 5 4-6-0 no.
73142 prepares to leave with the 10.50 express to Leicester.

Stewarts Lane Shed 31921
Maunsell W Class 2-6-4T no. 31921 was one of three class members employed at Stewarts Lane shed. The
engine arrived from Hither Green in August 1954 and remained until November 1960 when all were transferred
away, mainly to Eastleigh or Exmouth Junction.

Stewarts Lane Shed 31558
Ex-SE&CR Wainwright P Class 0-6-0T no. 31558 is shunting milk wagons at Stewarts Lane on 7 April 1951. The engine was a long-term servant at the depot.

Stewarts Lane 43121
Ivatt Class 4MT 2-6-0 no. 43121 travels southward with a freight train from Battersea Yard to Brent Sidings on 15 February 1958. The engine is seen from Stewarts Lane locomotive yard and is passing by the large furniture repository used by Harrods.

Stewarts Lane Shed 756

Built for the Plymouth, Devonport & South Western Junction Railway by Hawthorn Leslie & Co. in December 1907, no. 756 *A. S. Harris* was initially used to work mineral trains in Cornwall. The engine was later taken into L&SWR stock just prior to Grouping, then being sent around the SR system as a shed pilot. By the late 1940s no. 756 had reached Stewarts Lane and is seen here under the mechanical coaler on 7 April 1951. Withdrawal would soon occur in August.

Stewarts Lane Shed

Locomotives have been stabled at Stewarts Lane, also known as Battersea or Longhedge, since the LC&DR built the first shed in 1862. A new 16-track building was built in 1881 and standing outside this on 15 February 1958 are, left to right: no. 30919 *Harrow*, no. 73088, no. 34091 *Weymouth* and no. 73083.

Stratford Station 61223

Stratford station was not only on the main line to East Anglia, but the hub for suburban lines around East London, and remains a very busy interchange. Here, the 15.33 Liverpool Street to Lowestoft Central and Yarmouth South Town takes the fast line east behind Thompson B1 no. 61223 on 10 April 1958.

Stratford Shed 65462

GER Worsdell Y14 (LNER J15) Class no. 65462, which served in France during the First World War, had only 18 months to survive before being withdrawn when pictured on 18 February 1961 in Stratford shed yard. The locomotive—one of few fitted with a tender-cab—would not go to the scrapyard, however, as the Midland & Great Northern Joint Railway Society stepped in and took no. 65462 to the North Norfolk Railway.

Stratford Station 61611

The electrification of Stratford station for suburban services was instigated by the LNER in the mid-1930s, but was halted by the Second World War. After the end of hostilities the work continued and was completed in November 1949. Gresley B17 Class 4-6-0 no. 61611 *Raynham Hall* (built in August 1930, condemned during September 1959) passes under the wires with an express from Yarmouth to Liverpool Street on 10 April 1958.

Stratford Station 5365

Worsdell Y14 (LNER J15) Class no. 5365, built in October 1889, pauses at Stratford station on the up main line with a goods train. An original GER name board is still in evidence in this picture, taken 12 April 1947.

Stratford Station 64689

Hill's GER D81 Class (LNER J20) were erected in the two years prior to Grouping, and at this event 25 of them passed into LNER stock. At the time these 0-6-0s were the most powerful of the type at work in Britain, until Bulleid's Q1 Class appeared some 20 years later. No. 64689 is certainly not being taxed in bringing this cattle wagon from the direction of Temple Mills Yard on 5 December 1959.

Stratford Shed 8625

A large roundhouse shed was built by the Northern & Eastern Railway in 1840 and this was located to the north of Stratford station on the west side of the running lines. This was later absorbed by the GER and closed by the company when a new six-track structure was erected to the west of the above in 1871. A large 12-road building was constructed in 1887, thus allowing around 500 engines to be stabled at the depot. J69 No. 8625 Class 0-6-0T was one of approx. 70 based at Stratford when pictured in September 1946.

Stratford Station 70041

The 'Britannia' Pacifics were built by BR between 1951 and 1954, when 55 were in service. No. 70041 *Sir John Moore* left Crewe Works in March 1953 and proceeded to work from Stratford until February 1959 when a move to Norwich occurred. Stratford shed had usually about a dozen on the books until the latter date. Then all were transferred to East Anglia as the former depot was struggling to carry out maintenance of the locomotives. No. 70041 is seen with a relief express on 23 December 1959.

Stratford Works 7230

Y5 Class 0-4-0T no. 7230 was the final class member left in service when pictured on 28 September 1946, being employed at Stratford's Carriage Works. Despite having extensions added to the original coal bunker, this was evidently not enough!

Vauxhall Station 30321

Drummond's M7 Class 0-4-4T engines were introduced in 1897 to work L&SWR trains in and around the London area. A total of 105 were constructed up to 1911 and the majority emerged from Nine Elms Works, with no. 30321 being completed there in August 1900. The locomotive is seen on a journey from Clapham Junction to Waterloo with empty carriages for an express service.

Vauxhall Station 34022

With a number of problems emerging from Bulleid's original design, 60 of the 'Light' Pacifics were rebuilt with standard components. No. 34022 *Exmoor* was transformed towards the end of 1957, which was the first year of the rebuilding programme. The engine is coupled to the 14.20 Bournemouth to Waterloo express on 25 August 1962.

Vauxhall Station 30925

In the late 1920s the 'Schools' Class was designed to meet the need for a powerful engine which was to be used on the SR's passenger services and a total of 40 were built between 1930 and 1935. No. 30925 *Cheltenham*, pictured with the 17.00 Waterloo to Yeovil Junction, entered traffic in April 1934.

Vauxhall Station 443

Drummond T14 Class 4-6-0 no. 443 approaches Vauxhall station on the down line with a train of empty milk wagons on 24 April 1948. The milk had been removed from the tanks at the station to the United Dairies depot at the western side. The train then went to Waterloo to reverse before travelling back to Torrington, Devon. The engine was the first of the class to be built (in March 1911) and remained in service until May 1949.

Vauxhall Station 35017

By the end of the 1930s the SR required a new express passenger locomotive capable of hauling the company's heavy boat trains. The new C.M.E. O. V. S. Bulleid duly obliged and the first 'Merchant Navy' Class Pacific was in service for June 1941. A further 29 were built up to 1949; no. 35017 *Belgian Marine* was completed at Eastleigh Works in April 1945 (as no. 21C17). Photographed here with the 13.05 express from Bournemouth on 24th April 1948, the engine was being prepared for the exchange trials.

Vauxhall Station 30520

Vauxhall station was opened as a temporary stop on the L&SWR's Nine Elms to Waterloo extension line on 11 July 1848. The station was indeed short-lived as a fire destroyed the wooden buildings in 1856. This picture of Feltham-allocated H16 Class locomotive no. 30520 has been taken on 25 August 1962.

Vauxhall Station 30517
Another Urie H16 employed on empty stock work was no. 30517, which was also a resident at Feltham. The locomotive was constructed at Eastleigh Works in November 1921 and condemned in December 1962.

Vauxhall Station 42198
The number of lines into Waterloo was increased in the late 1880s and as part of this project Vauxhall station was completely renewed with three island platforms and ticket hall, which was placed centrally on the western platform. Two more running lines and a platform were installed at Vauxhall in the latter half of the 1910s as the L&SWR's electrification scheme came to fruition. Fairburn Class 4 2-6-4T is running at the south end of the station with empty carriages on 24 April 1948.

Victoria Station 70004
Immaculately presented 'Britannia' Pacific no. 70004 *William Shakespeare* moves out of Victoria station with the 'Golden Arrow' express Pullman service to Folkestone on 5 September 1953. This prestige train, which would continue as the 'Fleche d'Or' through France to Paris, had originated shortly after Grouping and was named in the late 1920s.

Victoria Station (East Side) 31408
The eastern side of Victoria station was opened by the LC&DR on 3 December 1860 and was shared with the GWR; the western side had been used by the LB&SCR from 1 October. Working at platform five is Maunsell N Class no. 31408.

Waterloo Station 475

Four months after Nationalisation and Urie H15 Class no. 475, at Waterloo's platform 15 with the 13.54 semi-fast to Basingstoke on 20 April 1948, is still identified as being under SR ownership, but by the end of the year this would be rectified. The engine had been constructed in March 1924 and remained in traffic until December 1961.

Waterloo Station 30453

N15 no. 30453 *King Arthur* was nominally a rebuild from Drummond's unsuccessful four-cylinder G14 Class and was transformed in February 1925. *King Arthur* poses here at platform 12 with the 14.54 stopping service to Basingstoke on 11 May 1959.

Waterloo Station 30773

The N15 'King Arthur' 4-6-0 Class was introduced by Urie for work on the L&SWR's express passenger services. Maunsell updated the design after Grouping and a further 54 were completed. No. 30773 *Sir Lavaine* was one of 30 built by the North British Loco and arrived on the SR during June 1925. The locomotive is seen at the end of platform 14 with the 10.54 express to Bournemouth West on Saturday, 24 June 1950.

Waterloo Station 414

Drummond L11 Class 4-4-0 no. 414's career would not last much longer when pictured in late June 1950, as withdrawal would occur in April 1951. The engine had been erected in July 1906 as part of 15 built during the year. A total of 40 were constructed between 1903 and 1907. The class was introduced to perform a mixed traffic role, but no. 414 is employed on empty stock duty here.

Waterloo (East) Station 916
The 13.15 Charing Cross to Margate express service stops at Waterloo (East) station, with Maunsell 'Schools' Class locomotive no. 916 *Whitgift* at the front of the train. The station was opened by the SER on 1 January 1869 as Waterloo Junction, being a short distance to the north east of the L&SWR's facilities. 'Junction' was removed from the title in 1935 but 'East' was not added until 2 May 1977.

Waterloo Station 46154
Rebuilt 'Royal Scot' no. 46154 *The Hussar* was another of the participants in the 1948 locomotive exchanges. The locomotive has been fitted with a 5,000 gallon tender from a WD 2-8-0 as there were no water troughs on the SR line.

Above: **Waterloo Station 22**

Thirty-five of Gresley's A4 Class Pacifics were built between 1935 and 1938 to handle the LNER's express passenger traffic. Of these only four of the later examples were fitted with Kylchap blastpipes and double chimney, the first being no. 22 *Mallard* when built at Doncaster Works (as no. 4468) in March 1938. The Kylchap A4s were specially selected to take part in the locomotive trials and *Mallard* is seen here arriving on a preliminary run from Exeter to Waterloo on 1 June 1948.

Opposite page, from top to bottom:

Waterloo Station 30339

L&SWR Drummond 700 Class 0-6-0 no. 30339 was constructed at Dübs & Co. in June 1897 and survived until May 1962. A total of 30 locomotives were built at the works to the design, which shared a number of features with the Caledonian Railway 0-6-0s produced by Drummond while he was Locomotive Superintendent of the company. The 700 Class were built to handle freight traffic, but no. 30339 has been relegated to moving empty carriages (for Farnborough Air Show) at Waterloo on 8 July 1950.

Waterloo Station D.E. 1

In the mid-1930s Maunsell investigated the possibility of purchasing three diesel-electric shunting engines for comparison against steam. English Electric agreed to supply the engines but the SR had to produce the frames etc. at Ashford. Three locomotives arrived back on SR metals in August and September 1937 and were employed in Norwood marshalling yards. After a year or so in service a saving of just under £2,000 was calculated compared with steam locomotives used on the same tasks. Shunter no. 1, while temporarily bearing an 'S' prefix, has been requisitioned from Norwood to assist with track relaying at Waterloo on 1 April 1948.

Above: **Waterloo (East) Station 34027**
The 15.08 Charing Cross to Deal approaches Waterloo East station behind Bulleid 'Light' Pacific no. 34027 *Taw Valley* on 11 May 1959. In the background, construction of the 'downstream building' of the Shell Centre progresses towards completion in 1961.

Opposite page, from top to bottom:

Waterloo Concourse
The L&SWR opened Waterloo station as Waterloo Bridge on 11 July 1848. The facilities were designed by William Tite. Waterloo was initially only meant to be a temporary terminus as the L&SWR wished to extend the line even further east to the city, but this did not come to pass and several additions were made at the station. By the beginning of the twentieth century the site needed rationalising and a wholesale rebuilding project was implemented. However, the work progressed slowly, being interrupted by the First World War, and was not completed until March 1922 at a cost of over £2 million. This busy scene was captured looking north-eastward along the concourse near platform 12 on 18 May 1964.

Waterloo Station Track Relaying with 419
Platforms three and four have been taken out of use during Monday, 19 July 1948, as track relaying is carried out close to the buffer-stops before an assemblage of onlookers. L&SWR Drummond L12 Class 4-4-0 no. 419 is assisting with the operation. The locomotive was one of a class of 20 constructed for express passenger services at Nine Elms Works in 1904-5; no. 419 lasted until November 1951.

Wembley Central Station 42183

5 May 1962 was FA Cup Final day and contesting the famous trophy at Wembley Stadium were Tottenham Hotspur and Burnley. In addition to trains arriving in London from the north, shuttle services were provided from Marylebone to Wembley Stadium station and at Euston to Wembley Central. Here, Fairburn Class 4 2-6-4T no. 42183 (built January 1949, withdrawn September 1966) arrives from Euston on the down slow line.

Wembley Central Station 42470

This local train arrives at Wembley Central on 5 May 1962 behind Stanier Class 4MT 2-6-4T no. 42470. The station was opened by the London & Birmingham Railway on 8 August 1842 as Sudbury. The title became Sudbury & Wembley in May 1882, but in November 1910 the latter place gained the honour of appearing first. From 5 July 1948 Sudbury was dropped and Wembley Central adopted as the station's name.

Wembley Central Station 45705
Blackpool-allocated Stanier 'Jubilee' Class no. 45705 *Seahorse* has arrived at Wembley with a fans' special. The locomotive would not return the supporters to Lancashire in jubilant spirits, however, as Burnley lost the match 3-1. No. 45705 had spent 20 years working in Yorkshire prior to being allocated to Blackpool in June 1956 and would be withdrawn from Newton Heath in November 1965 after 18 months at the depot.

Wembley Central Station 45229 and 44940
This supporters' charter train has travelled from Colne via Stockport behind two of Rose Grove shed's Stanier Class 5 4-6-0s. The leading engine is no. 45229 which was constructed by Armstrong Whitworth & Co. Ltd in July 1936 as part of 227 ordered from the company and featuring sloping throatplate fireboxes and domed boilers. Behind is no. 44940 and this was a later addition to the class in November 1945.

West Ealing 4919

This picture has been taken looking eastward to West Ealing station from a footbridge over the ex-GWR main line on 8 June 1962 and Collett 'Hall' Class no. 4919 *Donnington Hall* is seen travelling west with a parcels train. At this point, just to the left, the Greenford branch heads north to the former GWR and GCR joint line.

West Ealing Station

The GWR did not install West Ealing station until 1 March 1871 and at this time the title was Castle Hill. Just four years later Ealing Dean was added, remaining in use until six months before the start of the twentieth century. The station building, viewed from Drayton Green Road, was demolished in the late 1980s and replaced by a new structure.

West Ealing 2892
Collett '2884' Class 2-8-0 no. 2892, which has passed through West Ealing station and under St Leonard's Road bridge, heads into the capital on the slow line with a freight train on 13 April 1962. The locomotive was constructed at Swindon in April 1938 and would be in service until May 1963.

Willesden Junction Station 34101
Brighton-allocated rebuilt 'West Country' Pacific no. 34101 *Hartland* comes off the West London Line and would shortly be removed from this Hastings to Walsall express. An ex-LMS engine would take the reins and complete the journey up to the Midlands.

Above: **Willesden Shed 42221**

Both Fairburn Class 4MT 2-6-4T no. 42221 (in store) and Stonebridge Park power station were coming to the end of their operational lifespan when photographed on 25 November 1962. The locomotive (built in February 1946) had been made redundant by the recent electrification of the Tilbury line, but would be taken out of storage and sent north to Kirkby-in-Ashfield in May 1963. No. 42221 would find employment there until September 1964 when sent for scrap. Stonebridge Park had been constructed in the mid- 1910s as part of the LNWR's pioneering DC electrification project between Euston and Watford. Closure occurred in 1967 as National Grid began to power the line.

Opposite page, from top to bottom:

Willesden Shed 5699

The now-preserved 'Jubilee' Class locomotive, no. 5699 *Galatea*, is seen at Willesden shed on 27 April 1946 while still employed by the LMS. The engine, along with classmate no. 5667 *Jellicoe*, had worked a football special from Derby for the 1946 FA Cup Final, which was the first after the Second World War. A crew member, in their eagerness, has chalked: 'Up the Rams: Derby–3, Charlton–1'. However, the match would finish 4-1 after Jackie Stamps scored his second in extra time. These 'Jubilees' operated from April 1936 until November 1964 and from November 1935 to January 1965 respectively.

Willesden Shed 3561

Class 2F 0-6-0 no. 3561 rests between empty stock moves on 27 April 1946 at Willesden shed. The locomotive had been one of seven Class 2Fs to be fitted with carriage warming apparatus, at both the front end and tender end, after authorisation was given in early 1927. A number of the class were similarly treated, by both the MR and LMS, over the years when the engines' duties required the equipment. No. 3561 was specially employed on the empty carriage workings to and from Euston as a result of the feature being present.

Above: Willesden Junction Station 45704

The London & Birmingham Railway opened Willesden station during the first half of 1841, but the exact date is not clear. The facilities only lasted for under 25 years because the LNWR built a new station a short distance to the southeast on 1st September 1866. As the name implies there were several connections to other routes in the immediate vicinity: the North London Line, the West London Line and North & South Western Junction Railway line. The aforementioned two routes were carried over the main line and Willesden Junction High Level station was constructed and opened on 2 September 1867 to allow passengers to switch between the three lines. Further platforms were added to Willesden Junction station with the introduction of electric services from Euston to Watford in 1912, and later Bakerloo Line trains utilised these, which were considered a 'New' station by the LNWR. 'Jubilee' Class no. 45704 *Leviathan* is reversing down the up main line platform line on 5 May 1962.

Opposite page, below:

Willesden Junction 30929

This view, taken looking south-east from Willesden Junction station's main down platform towards the West London line, shows 'Schools' Class 4-4-0 no. 30929 *Malvern* running tender first. The class were fitted with 4,000 gallon tenders, but with some slight detail variants. No. 30929 was paired with a tender that had a sideways mounted toolbox and curved footstep backing plates when new in July 1934. Another slight difference was that the wheels could be either spoked or disc centred; *Malvern* has the former in this instance. Condemned in December 1962, the engine's mileage was 1,138,000.

Above: **Willesden Shed 1204**

The last C.M.E. of the LMS, H. G. Ivatt introduced his Class 2MT 2-6-2T design a short time before Nationalisation. Ten were constructed before the event, one being no. 1204 which is seen in Willesden shed yard while still quite new on 5 January 1947. However, by the end of the year the engine would be disposed of to Abergavenny. No. 41204 would spend the latter part of the 1950s and the first half of the 1960s working in the West Midlands and around the border with Wales before withdrawal in November 1966.

Willesden Junction 42099

A train of empty carriages (of which two are ex-LNER and designed by Gresley), passes through the main line station on 25 August 1962 behind Fairburn Class 4MT no. 42099. The locomotive was Willesden-allocated between June 1962 and March 1963, when moved to Watford where withdrawal was carried out during December 1964.

Willesden Junction Station 42234

From the late 1950s several improvement schemes were carried out at Willesden Junction station. The first involved the High Level portion as the platforms were arranged into a single island. This is just glimpsed above the locomotive, while out of view to the left were the platforms for the suburban services and Underground trains. The main line station would close from 3rd December 1962 as the West Coast Main Line was electrified.

Willesden Junction 45567

'Jubilee' Class 4-6-0 no. 45567 *South Australia* was built at the North British Loco's Hyde Park Works during August 1934, beginning work at Aston shed. The locomotives built by this company differed slightly from the original specifications through being fitted with larger bogie wheels, with increased wheelbase, and boilers made from nickel steel. The engine speeds through to Euston with a football special on 27 January 1962.

Willesden Junction Station 46431

H. G. Ivatt also produced a tender version of his Class 2MT design and 20 were erected for the LMS at Crewe Works before Nationalisation. No. 46431 was built at Crewe a short time later in December 1948 and the engine's career spanned 19 years. When pictured at Willesden on 25 August 1962, the locomotive was allocated to Watford.

Wimbledon 76030

Ivatt's Class 4MT 2-6-0 design served as inspiration for BR's design team when the plans were produced for the Standard Class 4MT 2-6-0s. Although, one alteration was carried out after trials with Ivatt Class 4MT no. 43027 highlighted the need for an improved arrangement for the chimney and blastpipe. A total of 115 were constructed between 1952 and 1957, with no. 76030 entering traffic in November 1953. The engine is seen at Wimbledon with the 17.12 from Basingstoke to Waterloo on 15 May 1964.

Wimbledon 35003

'Merchant Navy' Class Pacific no. 35003 *Royal Mail* was the third engine of the class to be built at Eastleigh Works on September 1941. A further 27 would be produced up to April 1949 and all would later be rebuilt between 1957 and 1959, with *Royal Mail* being transformed in August 1959. The engine was withdrawn in July 1967 with a mileage of 1,132,000—equivalent to nearly 5,000 return trips between Waterloo and Bournemouth!

Wimbledon 35016

The L&SWR completed Wimbledon & Merton station on 21 May 1838. Added subsequently were platforms serving the Wimbledon & Croydon line, which had a section jointly operated by the L&SWR and the LB&SCR from 1868. Only 12 years later the station buildings and entrance were moved a short distance to the north of Wimbledon Bridge. This scene was captured just to the west of Wimbledon station, from the footbridge accessed from Alt Grove, and shows 'Merchant Navy' Pacific No. 35016 *Elders Fyffes* (built March 1945 and withdrawn in July 1966) heading a relief express.

Wimbledon 73118

BR Standard Class 5MT 4-6-0 no. 73118 is at the head of another service to Basingstoke, this one being the 18.09 ex-Waterloo. As the locomotive was SR-allocated in the late 1950s, the name from a withdrawn 'King Arthur' Class, no. 30789 *King Leodegrance*, was bestowed in February 1960 and carried until withdrawal in the massacre of July 1967.

Bibliography

Bradley, D. L. *Locomotives of the Southern Railway Part One*. 1975.

Bradley, D. L. *Locomotives of the Southern Railway Part Two*. 1976.

Bradley, D. L. *Locomotives of the L.S.W.R., Part One*. 1965.

Bradley, D. L. *Locomotives of the L.S.W.R., Part Two*. 1967.

Bradley, D. L. *Locomotives of the L.B.&S.C.R.: Part Three*. 1974.

Bradley, D. L. *The Locomotives of the South Eastern and Chatham Railway*. 1961.

Brown, Joe. *London Railway Atlas*, 3rd edition. 2013.

Dow, George. *Great Central Volume Two: Dominion of Watkin, 1864–1899*. 1985.

Dow, George. *Great Central Volume Three: Fay Sets the Pace, 1900–1922*. 1985.

Ellaway, K. J. *The Great British Railway Station: Euston*. 1994.

Griffiths, Roger and Paul Smith. *The Directory of British Engine Sheds and Principal Locomotive Servicing Points: 1 Southern England, the Midlands, East Anglia and Wales*. 1999.

Jackson, Alan A. *London's Termini*. 1969.

Jackson, Alan A. *London's Local Railways*. 1978.

Hawkins, Chris and George Reeve. *An Historical Survey of Southern Sheds*. 2001.

Hornby, Frank. *London Suburban: An illustrated history of the capital's commuter lines since 1948*. 1995.

Pritchard, Robert and Peter Hall. *Preserved Locomotives of British Railways*, 16th edition. 2014.

Quick, Michael. *Railway Passenger Stations in Great Britain: A Chronology*. 2009.

R.C.T.S. *A Detailed History of British Railways Standard Steam Locomotives Volume One: Background to Standardisation and the Pacific Classes*. 2007.

R.C.T.S. *A Detailed History of British Railways Standard Steam Locomotives Volume Two: The 4-6-0 and 2-6-0 Classes*. 2003.

R.C.T.S. *A Detailed History of British Railways Standard Steam Locomotives Volume Three: The Tank Engine Classes*. 2007.

R.C.T.S. *A Detailed History of British Railways Standard Steam Locomotives Volume Four: The 9F 2-10-0 Class*. 2008.

R.C.T.S. *Locomotives of the L.N.E.R. Part 2A: Tender Engines–Classes A1 to A10*. 1978.

R.C.T.S. *Locomotives of the L.N.E.R. Part 2B: Tender Engines–Classes B1 to B19*. 1975.

R.C.T.S. *Locomotives of the L.N.E.R. Part 9A: Tank Engines–Classes L1 to N19*. 1977.

R.C.T.S. *Locomotives of the L.N.E.R. Part 9B: Tank Engines–Classes Q1 to Z5*. 1977.

R.C.T.S. *The Locomotives of the Great Western Railway Part Five: Six-Coupled Tank Engines*. 1958.

R.C.T.S. *The Locomotives of the Great Western Railway Part Eight: Modern Passenger Classes*. 1960.

Sixsmith, Ian. *The Book of the Royal Scots*. 2008.

Swift, Peter. *Locomotives in Detail Six: Maunsell 4-4-0 Schools Class*. 2006.

Thorne, Robert. *Liverpool Street Station*. 1978.

Townsin, Ray. *The Jubilee 4-6-0s*. 2006.

Walmsley, Tony. *Shed by Shed Part One: London Midland*. 2010.

Walmsley, Tony. *Shed by Shed Part Two: Eastern*. 2010.

Walmsley, Tony. *Shed by Shed Part Five: Southern*. 2008.

White, H.P. *A Regional History of the Railways of Great Britain, Volume 3 – Greater London*. 1963.

Wrottesley, John. *The Great Northern Railway: Volume 1 Origins & Development*. 1979. Wrottesley, John. *The Great Northern Railway: Volume 2 Expansion & Competition*. 1979.